Consultation
in Social Work

Consultation in Social Work

Alfred Kadushin

Columbia University Press New York
1977

Library of Congress Cataloging in Publication Data

Kadushin, Alfred.
    Consultation in social work.

    Bibliography: p.
    Includes index.
    1. Social service.   2. Social service—Team
work.   3. Medical consultation.   4. Psychiatric
consultation.   I. Title.
HV41.K22   361'.06   77-24345
ISBN 0-231-04124-1

COLUMBIA UNIVERSITY PRESS
New York   Guildford, Surrey

ENCORE ET TOUJOURS, À SYLVIA—
WITH WHOM MUCH IS PROBABLE;
WITHOUT WHOM LITTLE IS POSSIBLE

Contents

Preface

THERE HAS BEEN a growing demand for, and utilization of, social workers in indirect services, such as consultation. Despite this, training programs and training materials available to prepare practitioners for such responsibilities are limited. This text is an effort to meet the need for a systematic presentation of the essentials of social work consultation.

The number of social workers acting in the role of consultant is exceeded by the much larger number of social workers who find themselves in the role of consultee. There is a general lack of training for this role as well. A book on social work consultation can be an aid in the more adequate preparation of social workers in their more frequent role as consultees. Knowledge and understanding of the consultation process can help the consultee, as an active participant, to utilize the experience more productively. The book can be used at the bachelor's degree level of training as well as the master's and doctoral levels since it is, in effect, addressed to social work consultees, social work consultants, and consultees who plan to become consultants.

The text was developed over a seven-year period in teaching seminars in supervision and consultation, and refined in the leadership of institutes and workshops in social work consultation. The teaching experience was supplemented by practice experience as a consultant to child welfare agencies, government agencies, and schools of social work.

It also grew out of the work involved in writing a previous book on supervision—*Supervision in Social Work*.[1]

Supervision of social workers should be terminated as early as possible and the relationship between supervisor-supervisee converted into a relationship of consultant-consultee. A book on consultation is, consequently, a logical sequence to a book on supervision.

The book reviews the history and current situation of consultation in social work and analyzes the difference between consultation and other processes with which it might be, and often is, confused—i.e., supervision, collaboration, therapy, staff development. This is followed by a detailed specification of the situations encountered by social workers as consultants and as consultees. The major part of the book is concerned with an analysis of the consultation process, the sequential steps from contact through termination. It ends with a review of evaluation studies of consultation and a delineation of the more significant problems facing social work consultation. There is, throughout, a conscientious, if not exhaustive, effort to cite the relevant literature and to make maximum use of the limited empirical material available. Wherever possible, case material has been used to illustrate the substantive content. There is, however, little detailed case material available on social work consultation.[2]

While primarily concerned with process, the orientation of the book is that the rationale for consultation lies in the problem-solving help offered the consultee on the basis of a clearly defined expertise which the consultant brings to the situation.

[1] New York: Columbia University Press, 1976.

[2] After the book was in print, an excellent casebook on social work consultation became available. We are glad to be able to refer the reader to it as useful supplementary material: Alice H. Collins, Diane L. Pancoast, and June A. Dann, *Consultation Casebook* (Portland, Ore.: Portland State University, 1977; mimeo.).

Sexual designation of participants in the consultation event presents a problem. Rather than conform to the traditional solution of designating "consultant" as male and "consultee" as female throughout, we randomized the sexual designation of consultant and consultee. This results in some disconcerting shifts in pronouns in the text; the consultant being "he" sometimes, "she" at other times.

Most of the book was written during the period when the author was a Fellow at the Center for Advanced Studies in the Behavioral Sciences, Palo Alto, California. A fervent vote of thanks to the Center for providing the time and the freedom to "do one's thing" in a context which is eminently supportive of scholarly activity.

My thanks also to the hundreds of social work consultants who took the time and the energy to complete the prolonged questionnaire on which some of the book is based; to Myles Buckman, doctoral candidate at the University of Wisconsin, who assisted me in the survey; and to Jean Allen, who, unerringly, typed most of the manuscript.

My thanks and appreciation to John D. Moore, my friend and personal good shepherd, for lo these many years, at Columbia University Press, and to Dorothy M. Swart, who edited the book with unruffled professional competence, compassion, and understanding.

And my thanks and love to Micky, Tudella, and Duvie, who were there at the beginning and will, hopefully, be there at the end.

Consultation
in Social Work

Chapter One
History and
Current Situation

Consultation in social work is an old story, but it has only a short and recent history. The function was undoubtedly performed since the inception of social work as a profession. It is necessary, however, for self-conscious identification of a function to reach some level of explicit awareness before it is studied, examined, and reported on with any frequency. The function has to be given a name, an identity, a definition, and some beginning conceptualization so that people can recognize they are engaged in, let us say, consultation when they perform some recurrent kinds of activity. Until then the phenomenon has no history.

This did not happen for social work consultation until after World War II. It was only then that consultation, as an explicitly identified component of practice with some special distinctive attributes clearly differentiating it from other help-giving processes, began to emerge.

A forty-year index of articles that appeared in the *Social Service Review* between 1927 and 1966 lists only two entries under "consultation," both published after World War II (*Social Service Review*, 1968).

The index of the *Proceedings* of the National Conference of Social Work (formerly National Conference of Charities and Corrections) for the period 1874–1933 does not even include a listing for consultation (National Conference of Social Work 1935). A review of the National Conference presentations between 1933 and 1975 found only two very brief references to consultation during that period.

Consultation was not indexed in the *Social Work Yearbook* until the fifteenth edition (the *Encyclopedia of Social Work*) in 1965, although it did receive a brief mention by Grace White in the article on medical social work in the 1947 edition.

Historical Background

PSYCHIATRISTS IN SOCIAL AGENCIES

A number of different factors helps to account for the emergence of consultation as an identifiable social work function and activity. One consideration was the increasing use of psychiatric consultation by social work agencies after World War II. In this instance the social worker was the consultee, and there was concern on the part of the agencies for making most effective use of psychiatric consultation. As early as 1938 Moore discussed "an arrangement" for the use of psychiatrists in casework agencies which, combining clinical and educational functions, "may be broadly described as psychiatric consultation" (1938, p. 218).

By the early 1950s there was sufficiently wide use of psychiatric consultation by voluntary family service agencies to warrant both a study of the patterns of use of this resource (Family Service Association of America, 1953) and a position paper on psychiatric-social work relations in consultation (Family Service Association of America, 1956). The study in the use of purchased psychiatric consultation by a sample of 17 family service agencies scattered throughout the country was conducted in 1951. The agencies, with an aggregate casework staff of 629 workers, had used the services of 50 psychiatric consultants. "A relatively small proportion of the total agency case load was taken for consultation with the psychiatric consultants" (Family Service Association of America, 1953, p. 3)—over all, for the 17 agencies, about 1.7 percent of the total caseload. The major activity engaged in by the psychiatric consultant was focused on consultation with casework personnel on individual cases. This accounted for 64 percent of the consultation time. About 15 percent of the time was devoted to consultation with agency administrators regarding agency programs, and 11 percent was devoted to direct contact with clients. There is little in the reports to suggest that any significant amount of consultation time was employed in consultee-centered consultation—consultation focusing on the worker's contribution to the problem situation.

Purchase of psychiatric consultation time for the specific purpose of "seminar and teaching sessions" directed toward increasing the staff's knowledge of, and ability to use, psychiatric concepts was very limited, accounting for only 3 percent of the total consultation effort.

In addition to this attempt at systematic analysis of the activity of the psychiatric consultant, there was a sizable number of articles by agency consulting psychiatrists (Babcock, 1949; Bernard, 1954; Coleman, 1953; Goldman, 1940; Lifshutz, Stewart, and Harrison, 1958; Maddux, 1950; Thompson, 1957; and Van Ophuijsen, 1940) and by social work consultees in both voluntary and public agencies (Brody, 1951; Davis, 1957; Decker and Itzin, 1956; Levinson and Gomberg, 1951; Ormsby, 1950; Regensberg, 1951; Tannenbaum, 1951; Taylor, 1956).

In 1955 and again in 1957, special workshops on psychiatric consultation to social agencies were conducted at the annual meetings of the American Orthopsychiatric Association (Bettelheim, 1958; Boehm, 1956; Garrett, 1956; Kaufman, 1956;

Perkins, 1958; Riley, 1958; Stein, 1956; Wright, 1958). The content in most of these articles was mainly experiential, case-oriented reports or discussions of the administrative interprofessional relationships between the psychiatrist consultant and the social work consultee.

Criteria of case selection for consultation were presented. The procedure for implementing the consultation was codified, and the process of psychiatrist-social worker consultation was detailed. The qualifications of an effective psychiatric consultant to a social agency were delineated, emphasis being placed not only on competence in psychiatric expertise but also on competence in communication.

Cases for consultation were generally selected by the worker in conference with the supervisor. A summary of the case record was sent to the consultant in advance. In some instances the consultant also read the original case record. The summary review of the case situation might also include the specific questions the consultee wanted to have discussed. On occasion, but not routinely, the psychiatrist-consultant might request an interview with, or an observation of, the client who was the subject of the consultation. It was generally suggested that supervisors participate in the consultation not only in helping the worker to select and prepare the case for consultation, but as resource persons in the consultation conferences and subsequently in helping the worker to implement the consultant's recommendations. The caseworker whose case was discussed was responsible for a recording of the consultation. If they were of sufficient general interest, cases brought for consultation might be presented in a case conference format which included other members of the casework staff. In these instances the psychiatric consultant acted as a case consultant to the worker who brought the case and as a seminar leader for the other participants for whom this was a didactic teaching-learning experience.

The request for help implied a need for clarification of the psychodynamics of the case situation; assistance in establishing a diagnosis and formulating case treatment plans; further knowledge and understanding by the worker regarding psychodynamics, psychopathology, and technical problems such as transference, separation, termination, and so forth, encountered in case management; and a desire for reassurance and support. Coleman (1953) said that if the worker "can be assured, through the psychiatrist, that she is not remiss in carrying out her responsibilities and if she can come to understand the client's motivations and the limitations of casework or psychiatric help, then she can go on with her work job in a clarified reality atmosphere" (p. 253).

It was recognized that the psychiatric consultant brings "a special competence which makes him, with reference to the [social work] consultee, an expert. . . . it is the psychiatrist's knowledge of psychodynamics and of psychopathology and, in some instances, his skill in psychotherapy which are the content of his expertness" (Boehm, 1956, p. 241).

The consultation function of the psychiatric consultant was frequently broadened to a more formal group educational function involving lectures and "staff seminars on the psychiatric aspects of the development and deviations of personality" (Brody, 1951, p. 152).

The reports on the use of psychiatric consultation by social agencies frequently reiterated the contention that psychiatry and social work were complementary professions concerned with similar problem situations but approaching them from different vantage points and with different orientations. Social work was concerned with, and possessed expertise in, the social components of the client's situation; psychiatry was concerned with, and possessed expertise in, understanding the more explicit intrapsychic aspects of the client's situation. The social worker needed, then, to borrow the psychiatrist's specialized knowledge via consultation if he was to understand fully the client's problems.

The special interest of psychiatric social workers in the con-

sultation process was exemplified by a special institute sponsored by the psychiatric social work section of the National Association of Social Workers (NASW) which took place in 1959. This
resulted in the first substantial publication on consultation in
social work—*Consultation in Social Work Practice* (Rapoport,
ed., 1963). The orientation of the institute and of the subsequent
publication was much broader than the psychiatrist-social work
consultant-consultee relationship and was concerned with a general attempt to conceptualize the consultation process.

In 1960 the psychiatric social work section of NASW made
an explicit effort to define the role of the psychiatric social
worker in mental health consultation. The report noted that the
"consultant is considered to be an expert in one or more areas of
a profession and he has certain authority by virtue of his knowledge. His role is to impart the knowledge rather than to act himself." The special expertise of the psychiatric social worker in
mental health was identified not only in terms of "clinical content of mental health practice" but also of "community functioning, community organization and agency structure within the
community" (Woodward, 1960, pp. 27–28).

HOST SETTINGS AND SOCIAL WORK CONSULTATION
A second factor which contributed to the growing concern with
consultation as a distinctive social work process was the activity
of a specialized group of social workers operating in host settings. Medical social workers, school social workers, and social
workers in the court system acted as consultants to other professionals who had primary responsibility for the functions of the
host setting.

Among the earliest published material on social work consultation are the papers given by Bartlett (1942) and Van Driel
(1942) at a conference in 1942, sponsored by the National Association of Medical Social Workers.

White (1947) notes that medical social workers were used as

consultants to "help members of the medical team to understand the social aspects of illness and medical care" (p. 310).

Thomas (1955) discusses medical social work consultation to medical and paramedical personnel. She defines medical social work consultation as "the process of putting at their disposal for use in their own care of patients the social worker's special knowledge and understanding of social problems and social resources" (p. 4). Leader (1957) reviews the experience of medical schools in the use of social work consultants for the purpose of helping students learn interviewing techniques and the significance of social and emotional factors in illness. His article presents a detailed account of social work consultation to psychiatry in the Veterans Administration Hospital in Topeka. The social worker consultant contributed knowledge about social agency resources and procedures, the social meaning of illness and hospitalization, and the social consequences of illness and hospitalization. Warriner (1949) reports on psychiatric social work consultation to public health nurses, and Alt (1959), on medical social work consultation to doctors in a health insurance plan organization. In both instances the social worker helped the consultees to understand and more effectively use social agency community resources. Public health nurses

found resistance on the part of patients to use available medical and social resources and needed to develop work skills in dealing with it. While knowing which social agency could best serve the patient the nurses were sometimes at a loss to understand how best to present the patient's problem to the agency and the agency's service to the patients. (Warriner, 1949, p. 393)

School social workers at this time also engaged in consultation, in this case the consultees being public school teachers and school administrators (Sikkema, 1955).

EXPANDING PROGRAMS AND CONSULTATION

A third factor which was related to the growing visibility of social work consultation was the development of federally supported social welfare programs, starting in the late 1930s but accelerating after World War II. Davis (1956) points out that federal legislation regarding social welfare programs delineates

> certain basic legal requirements as to organization policies and standards for state agency and local unit operations, but that much of their program development and standard-setting is accomplished through the provision of consultative help. For example the Social Security Act requires not only that state agencies have a merit system, but that they report regularly and that administration be proper and efficient. This leaves the area of personnel administration, research, and staff training to be developed through consultative help which supplements line staff. (p. 115)

Thus, the development of large-scale public welfare programs funded by federal and state government, but with the direct-services personnel a county responsibility, leads to the development of a considerable apparatus for administrative review. Program requirements and guidelines were set by the funding agencies. Consultation, as part of administrative review, was offered to help state and county agencies understand and meet these requirements and guidelines. The need for such consultation was intensified as a result of frequent revisions in such requirements and guidelines. As a consequence, both federal and state governments developed a corps of consultants who visited with personnel in local agencies to explain and help with the implementation of program directives.

Specialized child welfare services, frequently implemented by large staffs the largest percentage of which had limited training, required consultation from more experienced trained social workers. Several articles reviewed the activity of child welfare consultants with less experienced social work consultees in public child welfare agencies (Arnold, 1941; Beck, 1945; Keith-Lucas, 1954; Smyth, 1960.). Baxter (1956) reports on adoptive program consultation to child welfare agencies. In these articles there is an attempt to distinguish between administrative supervision of a local agency by a state unit and consultation to the local agency by representatives of the state child welfare departments.

Rosenthal, a psychiatrist, and Sullivan, a social worker, offer the most detailed presentation available of the work of a social work consultant with social work consultees in a public child welfare agency. The report of a project in which psychiatric social workers offered consultation regarding the psychodynamic aspects of child welfare service situations contains one of the very few reports which include typescripts of tape-recorded interactions between the consultants and consultees (Rosenthal and Sullivan, 1959).

The 1962 amendments to the Social Security Act tended to result in an increased use of psychiatric consultants by public welfare agencies. The amendments placed greater emphasis on social services as the preferred approach to helping welfare recipients. The charge was directed to staffs composed largely of people with limited or no professional education in a personalized service. Effective implementation of such an orientation required both in-service training and consultative assistance. While such consultation had been offered earlier to public welfare staff in selected instances (Bush and Llewellyn, 1958) such programs were expanded in the 1960s (Liben, 1969). Rogawski (197-1) undertook a questionnaire survey in 1971 of psychiatric consultation to public welfare staffs. Three quarters of the forty-three states responding indicated that they had "individual or group consultation programs for their staff. Most frequently the consultation seemed client-centered, less often consultee-centered, and in only one-third of the states were psychiatrists invited to participate in administrative consultation" (p. 764).

Other kinds of recent legislative enactments have increased

the need for consultation to community-based institutions which have responsibility for offering service to those who are at risk for mental health services. Various states have mandated that public schools meet the full educational needs of every child no matter what the nature of his mental, emotional, or physical difficulty. The challenge has intensified the need for consultation on the part of school systems in meeting the legislative demand.

The process of maturation of professional services gradually leads to conditions which require more explicit concern with consultation. As standards of service are formulated and organizations are developed to monitor standards, consultation needs to be available to the agencies interested in being licensed or approved. The Family Service Association of America and the Child Welfare League of America are examples of national organizations that not only require their agency membership to adhere to minimal standards but also offer consultation to applicant and member agencies. Similarly, as standards were established for day care and nursing homes, consultation needed to be available to help service organizations understand and achieve the required standards.

COMMUNITY MENTAL HEALTH CONSULTATION

Perhaps the most salient, recent factor which relates to the intensification of concern with social work consultation grows out of the developments in community mental health rather than developments in social work more narrowly defined. The Mental Health Act of 1963, which provided federal funding for community mental health centers, is often cited as the event which gave powerful impetus to programs of consultation.

The 1961 report of the Joint Commission on Mental Illness and Health, which was in many respects the basis for the Mental Health Act of 1963, notes that:

A host of persons untrained or partially trained in mental health principles and practices—clergymen, family physicians, teachers,

probation officers, public health nurses, sheriffs, judges, public welfare workers, scoutmasters, county farm agents and others—are already trying to help and to treat the mentally ill in the absence of
professional resources. With a moderate amount of training through
short courses and *consultation* on the job, such persons can be fully
equipped with an additional skill as mental health counselors.

Persons fully trained in mental health professions—psychologists, social workers, nurses, family physicians pediatricians, or
psychiatrists, with particular interest in community service—should
be available for systematic consultation with mental health counselors. The basic functions of these consultants would be to provide
on-the-job training, general professional supervision of sub-
professional activities and the moral support and reassurance found
to be essential for most persons working with the emotionally
disturbed or mentally ill. (pp. xii–xiii)

This rationale for an expanded program of consultation was
further supported by the trend, during the 1960s and 1970s,
toward community-based psychiatric services and deinstitu-
tionalization of the mentally ill.

The concept of community psychiatry requires the greater
involvement of professionals associated with many different service groups in dealing with the mental health problems of their
clients. Community psychiatry suggests that mental health becomes the concern of many different services in the community
rather than the more exclusive concern of the core psychiatric
professions—psychiatry, clinical psychology, psychiatric social
work. The mentally ill, the potentially mentally ill, and the recovered mentally ill are not isolated but are encountered by a
wide variety of groups in the community. Changes in both the
ideology of mental hygiene and the actuality of the wider disper-
sion of mental health problems required a wider dissemination
of mental health information and related skills which, it was
thought, could be achieved through consultation.

Four of the five essential services required by law to be offered by the community mental health centers are concerned with direct-service—remediation efforts, inpatient service, outpatient service, and partial hospitalization services, including day treatment and emergency service. The fifth required service, consultation and education, is an indirect service concerned with the prevention of mental illness and the promotion of mental health. Thus the act officially identified consultation as a special service and gave it explicit recognition and support.

In 1975 this commitment was reaffirmed in the passage of public law 94–63, which broadened the mandate required of a comprehensive mental health center to include twelve basic services, one of which was, once again, consultation and education. The legislation authorized funds explicitly for this service.

By 1976 there were some 650 funded community mental health centers in operation, and in that year an additional $50 million was allocated by the federal government for the support of some 55 additional centers.

While the 1963 act is often cited as the initiation of nationwide mental health consultation services, the 1920s had witnessed the development of a similar kind of program but one which was not explicitly identified as consultation. In response to concern with the problems of juvenile delinquency, which were perceived as a manifestation of emotional disturbance in children, the Commonwealth Fund financed establishment of a series of demonstration child guidance clinics. Among the activities proposed for such clinics were functions which we now recognize as consultation:

> The demonstration clinics . . . were designed primarily not to provide treatment for children showing psychological problems but to enable a variety of other social, child welfare and educational organizations to handle problems of children in a more effective fashion. . . . It was apparent from the very beginning that a treatment service could never hope to meet service needs and that it would be necessary to develop techniques for educating the relevant settings to handle their own problems. (Levine and Levine, 1970, p. 277)

The child guidance clinic, as originally conceptualized in the Commonwealth Fund's program, was meant to be a vital force in the community closely interrelated with a variety of other agencies and the schools and designed to influence them. In today's terms the Commonwealth program would be a community mental health program (Levine and Levine, p. 231). The orientation of the program was that it is

> the institution and the social setting which were largely responsible for problems and that it is the institutional and social setting which should be changed in order to permit the individual to grow. . . . The answer to the institutional problem was to change the institution by educating personnel to think in a mental health framework (pp. 242, 244).

The public schools were then, as now, one of the principal targets for consultative efforts. The guidance clinic staff consulted in core conferences with teachers and school principals in an

> effort to change the attitude of the teacher toward this child and toward all other children in her care and the attitudes of the principal toward her teachers and the children in the school. We hope that the teacher may stop thinking about behavior difficulty in unit characteristics or as a moral obloquy and think of the behavior of the child as symptomatic of some underlying cause. (Blanton, 1925, p. 99)

It is clear from the descriptions of the activities engaged in

> that some of the early clinics were intimately involved in the community, that they made efforts to help community agencies handle their mental health problems, that there was a distinct preventative orientation and they saw as part of their function to install a mental health hygienic viewpoint in those who would have responsibility for the care of children. (Levine and Levine, 1970, p. 248)

Thus, in describing the activities of the child guidance clinic in Cleveland around 1924 it was noted that

> definite hours were set aside each week when a psychiatrist, a psychiatrist social worker or both met with workers from certain agencies to consult with them on cases which they found puzzling. More than two hundred cases were handled in this way apart from those actually referred for study at the clinic. Carrying educational work into the social agency by means of the worker's consultation service and through the cooperative handling of cases was a distinct gain. The setting up of small independent foci of mental hygiene work at strategic points, with the help from the clinic, further equipped the community to meet its whole problem and to get at behavior problems before they became court problems. (Stevenson and Smith, 1934, p. 43)

French (1940) notes that psychiatric social workers frequently acted as consultants to family service agencies. The extent of consultation to such agencies gradually diminished as most trained social workers became more psychiatrically oriented.

While juvenile delinquency was the original focus of concern of the child guidance clinic movement, it rapidly broadened its orientation to include mental health of children generally. Social workers were accepted as full members of the clinic team. The New York School of Social Work (now the Columbia University School of Social Work) was granted funds for the establishment of a special program to prepare psychiatric social workers for working in the clinics. By 1932 there were over eighty child guidance clinics in the country (Stevenson, 1934).

It might also be noted that sanction and support of consultation evidenced in the federal Mental Health Act of 1963 was in fact anticipated by state legislation passed in the 1950s. New York passed the first state community mental act in 1954 and was followed by California, Minnesota, and South Carolina which adopted similar legislation (Forstenzer, 1961). As a consequence of such action community mental health clinics were established through a grant-in-aid formula which provided federal support funds authorized by the National Mental Health Act of 1946. By 1962 such grants-in-aid for community mental health clinics totaled $6.75 million. The state legislation provided that a significant component of the community mental health centers' time was to be devoted to community consultation and education. For instance, the 1957 California act known generally as the Short-Doyle Act specified consultation as one of the five services reimbursable by the state. Consultation, to be reimbursable, was to be offered by qualified mental health personnel under general direction of a psychiatrist to schools, health and welfare agencies, recreation and group work agencies, family counseling services, and so on, in order to promote and broaden the mental health content of these services.

The identification of consultation and education, currently as in the past, as an essential service to the community to be provided by the mental health centers grew out of concern with placing greater emphasis on preventive procedures as contrasted with exclusive reliance on remediation in dealing with problems of mental health.

The premise was that "widespread application of mental health principles, especially to children, would substantially improve society, reduce crime and poverty and aid in reforming the criminal justice system, the schools and other institutions" (Musto, 1975, p. 57). While currently we are somewhat less naïve and more disenchanted with the possibilities of such an approach, there is a sizable component of this presumption in the expectations of the outcome from mental health consultation and education.

Community psychiatry also gained some impetus from the apparent ineffectiveness of the more traditional therapeutic approaches. It was felt that it was necessary to adopt procedures which were oriented to more decided efforts to mobilize community resources and institutions in promoting mental health.

Originally, too, the growth of interest in community mental

health consultation resulted from attempts to meet problems posed by the shortage of professionally trained manpower. As in supervision, the aim is to amplify the influence of those who have the most adequate professional training "through intermediation of large group of consultees, each of whom is in contact with many clients" (Caplan 1970, p. 21). Recent efforts to "empty" institutions and return residents to the community has resulted in the need for an extensive network of consultative help to a variety of community agents who have continuing responsibility for these groups.

The community mental health concern with consultation as an explicitly identified process has, as one of its most significant legacies, the conceptualization of the process by community mental health practitioners. The work of Altrocchi, Berlin, Rapoport, and, above all, Caplan is associated with such efforts. As a result of the influence on social work of these systematic efforts to develop a framework for consultation, social work consultation is often perceived primarily in mental health consultation terms.

Despite the rather limited volume of material specifically concerned with social workers in the role of either consultees or consultants, noted above, one of the early efforts to explicate the nature of the consultation process was attempted by a social worker, Charlotte Towle, in 1950 and 1951 (Towle 1970). In the workshop which she presented on consultation at that time, Towle detailed the function of a consultant, the principles of interpersonal consultation, and the nature and source of the consultation process. Another early effort which had widespread impact was a paper by Siegel (1955) which appeared in a pamphlet published by the Family Service Association of America. Toward the end of the 1950s Insley (1959), closely associated with Caplan's work, presented a general framework of social work consultation in a public health setting.

More recently, Rapoport (1971b) has made efforts to differentiate social work consultation in particular from mental health consultation in general.

The Current Situation of Social Work
Consultation

It was anticipated that as a consequence of community mental health legislation there would be a very decided increase in interest in, and jobs available for, social work consultants. Thus in recapitulating the history of social work practice in mental health between 1955 and 1969, Magner (1970) concludes that the

> social worker will continue to assume increasing responsibility for consultation. Indirect practice (one or more steps removed from the actual therapeutic or service contract) may constitute the major trend that has emerged in the past 15 years and may continue over the next 15 years. (p. 14)

It is difficult to document the validity of such a prognostication—and equally difficult to invalidate it. It is difficult to get hard reliable data which clearly indicate the extent to which social workers are engaged in consultation either as consultants or as consultees.

Despite the avowed support of consultation services by the federal government the available statistics regarding the actual implementation of such services suggest very limited interest on the part of mental health centers. Manpower utilization studies of mental health centers' personnel indicate least support for consultation among the services provided (Levinson and Reff, 1970). Other studies confirm the fact that only a very limited percentage of mental health center professional time is, in fact, devoted to consultation (Glasscote and Gudeman, 1969, p. 166; Perlmutter, 1974, p. 277).

In February, 1973, consultation-education services accounted, on the average, for 5.5 percent of total staff time of federally funded community mental health centers (Bass, 1974, p. 1). While consultation activities constitute a very modest component of the total services offered by these centers, social workers are the principal providers of consultation. Thus in February, 1974, 25.6 percent of consultation time was provided by center staff social workers as compared with 5.5 percent by center staff psychiatrists (U.S. Department of Health, Education and Welfare, 1975, Table 16).

Schools are by far the most frequent recipients of consultation services provided by community mental health centers. Over one third of the consultation and education effort was directed at school personnel consultees. About 10 percent of consultation-education services went to welfare agencies and alcohol and drug abuse agencies combined, and another 9 percent went to law enforcement personnel. Consultation concerning the aged commanded the smallest percentage of consultation-education staff time, about 3 percent (Bass, 1974, p. 3).

In order to obtain some indication of the social work involvement in consultation we requested from NASW a list of members who, in 1975, cited consultation as their primary job responsibility. The Association provided a list of some 980 social workers—about 1.5 percent of the total membership. That only a limited percentage of NASW membership is engaged primarily in consultation is confirmed by a similar, more recent, statistic offered by Fanshel (1976) in a review of the most recent computer runs of NASW members.

It may be that most social workers do have some experience with consultation. However for most of them this may be an infrequent event not centrally related to their primary job responsibilities. Thus, Smith (1975) contacted forty-eight 1965 graduates of the University of Utah School of Social Work, some ten years after their graduation. Seventy-five percent reported having had consultant experience. Most of those with experience as consultants were in psychiatric facilities. School personnel were the consultees most frequently offered social work consultation. However a single, time-limited experience during the ten-year period would have been sufficient to include a respondent in the statistics as a consultant.

Some clue as to the changing state of affairs is given by a study of the child welfare delivery system in twenty-five states in 1976 (Child Welfare League of America, 1976). This indicates that "a number of states have specialists giving consultation to local units in certain program areas such as adoption, foster care, and protective service. Many states report too few specialists, especially in view of the minimum level of skill and training of the front line workers and supervisors" (p. 220). The mid-level field consultation and specialist level personnel, who are often regionally located, have been diminished or eliminated in a number of states, often for fiscal reasons. State units had the responsibility of providing expert consultation to operating units. These functions were frequently

> performed by the state office for local units or by regional areas for local ones. . . . Outside expert organizations such as national clearing houses, specialized centers (e.g. The Denver Abuse Center) or major voluntary agencies with particular expertise are often used to provide significant consultation special program areas.
>
> Very few states expressed satisfaction at either the number of consultants or the range of consultation available to direct service personnel despite a range which spread from legal to nutrition to home management and maintenance. The most frequently mentioned lack was for adequate legal counsel for staff. (p. 111.61)

There are three other approaches that one might follow in attempting to obtain a picture of current social work consultation: (1) recapitulation of the recent articles devoted to consultation which have appeared in the social work literature; (2) a review of the extent of formal education for consultation in the curriculum of schools of social work; and (3) a summary of recent advertisements for social work consultants.

A review of *Social Work Abstracts* since its first publication in 1965 through 1976 indicates a total of ten citations under "consultation" from all of the social work periodicals during that period (Bell, 1975, 1976; Green, 1965; Kane, 1966; Macarov *et al.*, 1967; May, 1970; Nir, 1973; Schild, Scott, and Zimmerman, 1976; Simon, 1966; Williams, 1971). There has been, in addition, a scattering of articles written by social workers about social work consultation which have appeared in other than social work publications (Core and Lima, 1972; Cowen, Trost, and Izzo, 1973; Daggett *et al.*, 1974; Frankel and Clark, 1969; Horn *et al.*, 1969; Perlmutter, 1974; Perlmutter and Silverman, 1973; Rabiner and Sieberberg, 1970; Signell and Scott, 1972; Townsel, Irving, and Stroo, 1975; Wood, 1973).

It seems fair to say that the recent social work literature does not appear to reflect widespread, intense interest in social work consultation. No text on social work consultation has previously been published. A book on mental health consultation published in 1972, written by a psychiatrist, included the collaborative effort of a social worker, Rose Green, Professor Emeritus, University of Southern California (Beisser and Green, 1972). However, it might be noted that a very modest number of Ph.D. theses on consultation has been completed by social workers in doctoral programs in schools of social work (Aiken, 1957; Erickson, 1966; Kindelsperger, 1958; Mazade, 1972; Polenz, 1970; Smith, 1975).

A recapitulation with regard to the place of consultation content in the social work curriculum is equally revealing. As early as 1951 the medical social work section of NASW identified consultation as a content area which should be included in a program of education for medical social work. However, a thirteen-volume social work curriculum study by the Council on Social Work Education, published in 1959, made only one reference to consultation in the introductory volume and a few references in Volume 4, which was devoted to community organization. The 1962 curriculum policy statement of the Council made passing reference to consultation in listing the objectives of a curriculum in social work administration. The policy statement indicated that it was desirable that master's degree students, majoring in administration, be helped to "become familiar with administrative organization and method, particularly in relation to the functions of policy formation decision-making, supervision and consultation" (Council on Social Work Education, 1962, p. 6). Smith (1975) surveyed the programs of forty-four graduate schools of social work to determine course offerings covering content in social work consultation. Only fourteen schools, 32 percent, offered a specific course in consultation in 1975. Thirteen other schools (30 percent) "offered some content on consultation in courses that carried supervision in the name of the course" (p. 93). Thus the graduate social work curriculum also suggests a modest, limited interest in social work consultation.

It might be instructive to note that social workers seeking training in consultation have enrolled in special programs conducted under the aegis of public health or community mental health facilities—Harvard School of Public Health; Columbia University School of Public Health; the Center for Training Community Psychiatry, Berkeley; and the Center for Training in Community Psychiatry, Los Angeles.

A review of advertisements for social work consultants appearing in the NASW *Personnel News* and in such periodicals as *Social Casework* and *Child Welfare* between 1975 and 1976 uncovered fewer than twenty such advertisements. In a few instances the ad was for a social work consultant designated as such, as in the following:

> FIELD CONSULTANT. National accrediting agency seeks M.S.W. to provide consultation on specific problems such as programs, services, staffing and board function to agencies and communities. Consultant must make indepth studies of total agency operations. Must have minimum 8 years' experience in child welfare services and in administration. All staff based in New York; one-third to one-half travel time required throughout the U.S. and Canada. Starting salary up to $24,000.

MEDICAL SOCIAL CONSULTANT for statewide crippled children's program. Multidisciplinary practice. Assignments in regional offices. Requirements: M.S.W. and 3 years' experience.

More frequently the advertisement listed consultation as one of a number of functions which needed to be performed:

PSYCHIATRIC SOCIAL WORKERS (2) for immediate openings. M.S.W. required. We are seeking people with a great deal of initiative to perform wide range of community mental health functions. This includes direct services such as individual, group, and family therapy; program development in the initiation of a children's or aftercare service; consultation with other agencies; and supervision. We are a small outpatient mental health clinic moving to become a comprehensive community mental health center.

CLINICAL SOCIAL WORKER II. Current opening in new children's services program designed to provide full range of psychotherapeutic services for children under 12 and to develop community-oriented programs in consultation and prevention. Requirements: M.S.W. and 2 years' experience in children's treatment programs (medical or psychiatric social work). Salary range $12,684–$15,432.

EXPERIENCED MENTAL HEALTH WORKER. Rapidly developing comprehensive community mental health center which serves 4-county area in scenic mountain region of North Carolina needs experienced clinician to work in crisis intervention team. Prefer M.S. psychologist or M.S.W. social worker with several years' experience in direct service, preferably in community mental health setting. Opportunity to work with other treatment programs, community consultation, and outreach. Salary dependent on experience.

Summary

Despite social workers' involvement with consultation over a long period of time, explicit identification of social work consultation as a separate process was not evident until after World War II. As a result of growing collaboration with psychiatry, the expansion and specialization of social service programs and the development of community psychiatry, a greater effort was made to give consultation a clear visibility and identity. The current situation, as suggested by professional degree programs, personnel ads, and the periodical literature, indicates that consultation as a social work process is, as yet, a matter of limited interest and concern to the profession.

Chapter Two

Defining
Social Work Consultation

The variety of definitions available in both the social work literature and the literature of other human service professions recur-
rently points to some significant, supposedly differentiating,
aspects of consultation. Consultation is regarded as an interactional helping process—a series of sequential steps taken to
achieve some objective through an interpersonal relationship.
One participant in the transaction has greater expertise, greater
knowledge, greater skill in the performance of some particular,
specialized function, and this person is designated *consultant.*
The *consultee,* generally a professional, has encountered a problem in relation to his job which requires the knowledge, skill,
and expertise of the consultant for its solution or amelioration.
Consultation is thus distinguished from other interpersonal interactional processes involving the giving and taking of help,
such as casework, counseling, psychotherapy, by virtue of the
fact that its problem-solving focus is related to some difficulties
encountered in performing job-related functions and by virtue of

the fact that the identity of the consultee is generally restricted to someone engaged in implementing professional roles.

The immediate objective to be achieved by the interaction of consultant and consultee is that the consultee is enabled to deal more effectively with his work-related problem. The ultimate objective of consultation is the same as supervision—more efficient, effective service to agency clients.

An intermediate objective relates to the professional development of the worker. As a consequence of having learned how to deal with some specific problem with the help of the consultant, the consultee is subsequently better prepared to deal with similar problems.

The intended target for change resulting from the consultant's interventions may be the client, the consultee, or the system in which both client and consultee operate. The consultee may be an individual, a group, or a community.

The consultant has no positional administrative authority with reference to the consultee. The consultee is not administratively accountable to the consultant and is, furthermore, free to use or reject the results of the consultation. The relationship is entered into voluntarily by both participants.

The consultant does not offer a service directly to the clients. His impact on the clients is mediated through the worker offering the direct service. For this reason consultation, like supervision, is regarded as an indirect, nontreatment service. "The consultation is for the consultee's use in behalf of a third party" (Gilmore, 1962, p. 2), either individual client, group, community, or agency. As an indirect service, consultation is a "filter-down" procedure in which the positive effects on the consultee's professional functioning will ultimately have impact on the client.

A listing of some representative definitions of consultation from the human services literature reflects these considerations:

> Consultation is the process of interaction between two professional persons—the consultant who is a specialist and the consultee

who invokes the consultant's help in regard to current work problems with which he is having some difficulty and which he has decided are within the other's area of specialized competence. (Caplan, 1970, p. 219)

Consultation is a process whereby expertness in knowledge or skill is made available for the purpose of help with the solution of a problem by the provider of consultation to the recipient of consultation, the latter assuming the responsibility for seeking the consultation and for the use, non-use or partial use of the fruit of consultation. (Boehm, 1956, p. 241)

Professional consultation involves a process of planned change by which expert knowledge and skills are utilized in a relationship between consultant and consultee (individual, group or organization) for the purpose of enabling the consultee to increase, develop, free or modify his knowledge, skills, attitudes and/or behaviors toward the solution of a current or anticipated work problem; and secondarily for enabling him to be more effective in preventing or solving similar problems in the future. (Gorman, 1963, p. 28)

[Consultation is a] helping process which invokes the use of technical knowledge and professional relationships with one or more persons. Its purpose is to help consultees to carry out their professional responsibilities more effectively. (Insley, 1959, p. 216)

Expertise as an
Essential Component of Consultation

One of the principal characteristics of the consultant, repeatedly noted above, is the fact that he has some identifiable, established expertise. The dictionary definition of consultation, "to give expert advice," calls explicit attention to this key consideration. Webster defines "consultant" as a person who "gives expert professional or technical advice regarding matters in his field of special knowledge or training."

Additional definitions of consultation which might be cited further emphasize this. Thus, Brockbank (1968) speaks of consultation as related "to the consultant's specialized area of knowledge" (p. 267). Aiken (1965) defines consultation as a "process wherein one professional is asked to give advice or instruction to another in selected areas of knowledge in which the former is expert" (p. 46), and Smith (1975) regards consultation as "a vehicle by which individuals with identifiable expertise can share expertise" (p. 2).

What logically follows from this is that there is no "consultant" per se much as there is no "supervisor" per se. The "consultant" as a specialist-expert in some profession comes with the professional title prefacing the consultant title. There is a "psychiatric consultant," a "nursing consultant," a "legal consultant," a "social work consultant," an "engineering consultant," and so forth, but no such thing as a "consultant" per se. To say the word is to suggest expertise, which immediately raises the question, "In what?" One needs to be an expert in something before one can become a consultant—or be recognized as one.

As Seigel (1955) says: "The consultant, as a specialist, is expected to have broad knowledge and understanding of a specific area. . . . To be helpful, the consultant must first of all have the sturdy base of knowledge in his own specialty" (pp. 112–113).

She is seconded in this by Kiester (1969), who says that since "consultation is expert counsel or technical assistance in the solution of a problem . . . knowledge both general and specific of the subject matter about which one is consulting is obviously the prime requisite to effective consultation" (p. 36).

School of social work faculty members, interviewed in a study concerned with consultation content in the social work curriculum, clearly endorse the contention that "expertise in the practice of Social Work and its specialties was needed prior to the development of expertise in the consultation process itself" (Smith, 1975, pp. 101–2).

The principal, prime, and irreducible minimum essential prerequisite for a consultant is specialized expertise in the area he purports to represent. He would not be called in, or allowed in, to offer consultation unless he was perceived as having some identifiable, defined expertise. Furthermore, a specific, identifiable expertise on the part of the consultant is necessary if the perspective consultee is to know whom to contact in order to obtain the help he needs. A "consultant" without further identification cannot be related to a problem which might be primarily medical or legal or psychiatric.

There are apparent contradictions to the contention that specialized expertise is an essential prerequisite for consultation. Some firms are identified as consulting organizations without further specification. In these instances, the consulting firms, having no further identification, seek consulting assignments and then hire, if necessary, professionals who have specific expertise in the area of the assignment. This is characteristic of the procedures employed by such firms as Arthur D. Little, Peat Warwick and Mitchell, Booze Allen and Hamilton, and the Rand Corporation, all of which are engaged in the business of consultation (Guttman and Willner, 1976).

In some instances, the emphasis on expertise is not tenable because the nature of the relevant expertise is not easily identified or open to unambiguous validation. Thus, while the expertise of the brain surgeon or computer designer is clear on the basis of credentials, esoteric knowledge and, ultimately, observable activity, the expertise of the mental health consultant is not so easily and unquestionably established. Almost any reasonable, intelligent person with some general advanced educational credentials can, with sufficient chutzpah, present himself as a consultant for a wide variety of problematic interpersonal situations.

There is a more significant apparent contradiction to the emphasis on the necessity for expertise as a prerequisite for effective consultation in the orientation to consultation which gives primary emphasis to process as the most important contribution of the consultant. An orientation which gives process priority presumes that the consultee, individual, group, or organization,

knows how to solve its particular problem or knows how to get help
in solving them but that it often does not know how to *use its own
resources effectively* either in initial problem solution or in implementation of solutions . . . that inadequate use of internal resources
or ineffective implementation result from process problem. . . .
People fail to communicate effectively with each other or develop
mistrust or engage in destructive competition. . . . The job of the
process consultant is to help the organization to solve its own problems by making it *aware of organizational processes* of the consequence of these processes and of the mechanisms which can be
changed. The process consultant helps the organization learn from
self-diagnosis and self-intervention . . . where the standard consultant passes on his knowledge; the process consultant is concerned
with passing on his skills and values. (Schein, 1969, pp. 134–35)

The consultee knows the answer to her problem, but she has either failed to define it correctly or is psychologically blocked
from recognizing the solution (Rogers, 1973).

A psychiatrist consultant argues that "the major contribution of the consultation procedure lies not in the addition of any
new dynamic concept but in the process of encouraging, stimu-
lating and essentially freeing the caseworker to review and rein-
tegrate knowledge and hence more effectively to use the skills
and concepts which he already possesses" (Kaufman, 1956,
p. 227). In effect, the consultant "helps the caseworker find out
what he already knows." The consultant facilitates the
emergence of problem solutions rather than bringing an expert's
knowledge of problem solutions to be offered the consultee as
information, opinion, suggestion, and advice. Consultee and
consultant are colleagues, peers, struggling jointly to solve a
problem. The consultant's responsibility is to help the consultee
mobilize his own resources for more effective problem-solving.

Emphasis on process, as against content, legitimizes the
entry of a consultant into any situation regardless of whether he
knows anything about the content of the problem. This orientation suggests that the success of consultation is primarily depen-

dent on the interpersonal skills of the consultant and only secondarily on an expert's knowledge of the problem.

The process orientation does not, however, contradict the contention that the consultant has to bring some high level of expertise to the consultation. The consultant who claims no expert knowledge of the problem, no expert experience with possible solutions, must still bring considerable expertise in the process of facilitating the formulations of solutions on the part of the consultee. Acting as a kind of process gynecologist bringing to life the solutions the consultee did not know he had in him, requires an expert knowledge of interpersonal relationships and considerable psychodynamic skill in helping the consultee to effect interpersonal and intrapersonal change. It requires all of the very specialized expertise needed by change agents who claim to be able to help people change.

Schein's (1969) description of the process consultant at work in dealing with organizational problems and the reports of other process consultants (Beckhard, 1966; Bourn, 1973; David, 1967; Golembiewski and Blumberg 1967) indicate the need for expert skill in diagnosing organizational problems and the dynamics of group interaction so as to facilitate communication between groups at different levels of the hierarchy. Understanding the patterns of organizational decision-making, initiating and managing growth-producing interpersonal situations, the process consultant needs to be expert in the utilization of such procedures as sensitivity group leadership, role playing, brainstorming, survey feedback, derivation conferences. He needs an expert's knowledge of organizational psychology and organizational sociology. A process consultant who brings an expert knowledge of, and skill in, the use of process only is an expert indeed. With regard to the help he is called upon to provide, he is no more a colleague-peer of the consultee than is the more traditional "expert" consultant. Despite the emphasis on a spirit of "coordinate nonhierarchical interdependence" in the consultant/consultee relationship the consultant is more expert with regard to some competencies relevant to solving the problem the consultee faces than is the consultee. Even if the consultant is only *primus inter pares*—first among equals—he is still first.

It might be said further that the obligation for expertise on the part of the process-oriented consultant goes even beyond this. The consultant has a higher probability of being effective if, along with his specialized expertise in process, he also brings some familiarity with the particular kinds of substantive problems faced by the consultee. Haylett (1969) points to this when she says:

> Expertise in various specialized content areas in addition to competence in the consultative process is desirable. . . . Although the essence of the consultation process is to help the counselee use his own expert knowledge more effectively, the transaction is significantly enhanced when the consultant is also an expert in the mental health aspects of the kinds of clients that are likely to be discussed. (p. 296)

In criticizing the emphasis on expertise as the most relevant orientation for social work consultation, Rapaport (1971a) characterizes it "as essentially an elitest model of consultation which maximizes the power and influence" of the expert (p. 224). Rapaport called for a more collaboratively oriented approach to consultation "with emphasis on role modeling and learning via a socialization model approach." This approach also requires expertise on the part of the consultant although it may be a different kind than the more content-focused expertise traditionally described. The consultant has to know the kinds of behavior he seeks to model and be skillful enough to implement them if he is to act as a role model, and he needs to have an expert knowledge of the content of his socialization teaching if he is to teach it effectively to the consultee. What is changed is not so much the question of whether or not the consultant is "expert" in relation to the consultee but rather the nature of the content to be communicated and the procedures for communicating it. Once again, it seems to me, we come to some clearly identifiable expertise as being a principal attribute of the consultant.

Distinguishing
Social Work Consultation
from Other Types

The definitions which have been presented and the discussion up to this point have attempted to explicate what is distinctive about consultation as a unique process. Within the genus "consultation," however, there needs to be a more precise delineation of what distinguishes social work consultation from other kinds of consultation.

There is a limited number of definitions of mental health consultation, a rubric which includes social work, but fewer definitions of social work consultation per se. In both instances, the general definition is made specific to the particular kind of consultation by merely noting that the consultation is done by a mental health worker or a social work professional in relation to mental health or social work problems. For example, MacLennan, Quinn, and Schroeder (1975) define mental health consultation as

> provision of technical assistance by an expert to individual and agency care givers related to the mental health dimensions of their work. Such assistance is directed to specific work related problems, is advisory in nature and the consultant has no direct responsibility for its acceptance and implementation. (p. 5)

Hitchcock and Mooney (1969) similarly define mental health consultation as "an interaction between a mental health specialist, the consultant, or consultees, who believe they have a work problem which can benefit from the expertise of a mental health specialist" (p. 353).

And Haylett and Rapoport (1964) define mental health consultation as "a process of interaction between a mental health professional and one or more consultees for the purpose of increasing the consultee's awareness of and ability to manage the mental health components of his work" (p. 324). Lipowski (1976), who deplores the "tendency to extend and dilute the concept" and role of mental health consultant "to that of peripatetic human engineer or all around fixer of faulty human functioning (be it individual, group or organization) of any kind and in every setting" (p. 7), defines psychiatric consultation in more specific terms as the "provision of expert advice on the diagnosis, management and prevention of mental disorders by specially trained mental health professionals at the request of other health professionals and within the constraints of available knowledge and techniques" (p. 4).

In moving from mental health consultation to more specifically social work consultation, one finds the same tendency to differentiate merely on the basis of naming the professional designation of the consultant. Smith (1975) defines social work consultation as "the formal process wherein a social worker with an identified area of expertise attempts to help another professional or paraprofessional person (or group) to find alternative solutions to an identified problem with the total responsibility for a decision being left to the consultee" (p. 4).

Neither of the definitions of consultation which appear in the first and second editions of the *Social Work Encyclopedia,* which include a separate listing for "consultation," goes beyond a general definition to specify what differentiates social work consultation in particular from consultation in general. Rapoport (1965) defines "consultation in social work" as

a problem-finding process wherein a more knowledgeable professional consultant gives information and help to a less knowledgeable professional, the consultee, in order to strengthen him in his designated professional role by increasing his knowledge and skills, modifying his attitudes and behavior so that his specific problem may be solved, or generally enhancing his work performance for the ultimate benefits of the client he serves. . . . The consultant's authority rests on his status as an expert both in specialized knowledge of the field and skill in the use of consultation method. (p. 214)

In the second edition of the *Encyclopedia,* Rapoport (1971*b*) defines "consultation in social work as a professional method of problem-solving involving a time-limited purposeful contractual relationship between a knowledgeable expert, the consultant, and a less knowledgeable professional worker as the consultee."

In a subsequent review of Caplan's book on mental health consultation, Rapoport (1971a) criticizes the tendency to equate "mental health consultation" with consultation in general. She then goes on to distinguish between mental health consultation as described by Caplan in his book and social work consultation. She points to the fact that Caplan presupposes a one-to-one relationship between a consultant and a voluntary consultee in which the consultant is

a skilled diagnostician and therapist who uses this knowledge, transferred and adapted, to deal with sensitive emotional blocks, essentially via the method of displacement, without getting into a therapeutic relationship, which would be a clear violation of the contract and intention.

The reality in social work, and perhaps in the practice of community psychiatry as well, is that most consultation is done via group methods for the sake of reaching larger numbers for problem-solving and for its educational effects, that much social work consultation is nonvoluntary in nature and built into some mandatory or legislative expectations in regard to standard-setting, with the possibility of applying sanctions. . . . The idiosyncratic work problems, though important, need to be balanced by attention to the complex social-system problems that beset many bureaucratic organizations, whether large or small, problems that stem from organizational and structural inadequacies, problems of personnel and morale, or problems growing out of confusion of purpose and direction in keeping with changing and increasingly vociferous community demands for more relevant services and responses.

Dr. Caplan's model . . . . tends to stress a clinically rather than socially oriented approach to problem-solving.

The statement points to some of the structural differences between mental health consultation and social work consultation and hints at the differences in content which are the concern of the two different kinds of consultation.

On occasion a specialized social work group has formulated a definition of consultation relevant to its field of practice which identifies the differentiating content of the consultation it offers. Thus Siegel (1955) quotes a definition of medical social work consultation as

an advisory service to other professional personnel to: enlarge and deepen their understanding of the social and emotional difficulties which, in the discharge of their special responsibilities may be found to interfere with their efforts to help people achieve and maintain health; to help them deal more effectively with such factors in a way that will be appropriate to their function. (p. 99)

The definition indicates the specific content areas of concern in medical social work consultation in particular. Similarly, Austin and Kosberg (1976) offer a definition of social work consultation in nursing homes. They define such consultation "as the provision of technical assistance directed to specific work related problems, advisory in nature, by a professional social worker with a range of consultation skills to the staff and administration of long term facilities" (p. 6).

Synthesizing the general definitions of consultation and the material available on social work consultation, the following definition of social work consultation is proposed: Social work consultation is a problem-solving process in which help, purely advisory in nature, is offered by the social work consultant to a consultee (individual, group, organization, community) faced with a job-related problem. The problem with which the social work consultant is called upon to help has a social work component. The social work consultant brings to the consultation that expertise which derives from specialized social work education and practice.

A more precise delineation of the components of social work consultation will follow in Chapter 3.

Distinguishing Social Work Consultation from Related Processes

In addition to defining social work consultation there is a need further to distinguish social work consultation from other social work processes with which it might be and is, in fact, often confused. This section is concerned with distinguishing social work consultation from social work supervision, social work staff development and in-service training, psychotherapy and collaboration.

SUPERVISION

If the key consideration which defines consultation is expert help to the consultee with some problem encountered on the job, the danger of confusing consultation with supervision is apparent. After all, the supervisee comes to the supervisor for help with social work job-related problems in recognition of the fact that the supervisor is a more expert social worker. What, then, distinguishes the consultant from the supervisor?

One distinction relates to the temporal aspects of supervision as compared with consultation. Supervision is continuous;

consultation is on an *ad hoc* basis, as particular problems are encountered. The supervisor is responsible for a continuing relationship with the supervisee, helping him deal with the problems on the job. The consultant is generally called in intermittently to deal with special problems.

Because discontinuity is characteristic of consultation, this determines the kinds of problems for which consultation might most appropriately be sought. Generally, they are or should be, clearly defined, clearly circumscribed, and delimited problems which can be dealt with in a limited span of time. This is not to say that contact between a consultant and an agency may not be continuous. It often is. But each time the consultant comes he may, and often does, deal with a different problem. In this sense consultation is discontinuous, requiring the selection of tasks for consultation which differs from the selection of tasks appropriate to the continuity of supervision.

The consultant's contact with the consultee is not only limited from the point of view of time but also limited in scope. The consultant is concerned with only a limited segment of the worker's caseload; the supervisor is concerned with the whole range of the worker's performance.

The sole and exclusive focus of the consultant's concern is on helping the consultee with the work-related problem he brings. Supervision, on the other hand, inevitably has a more diffuse focus. While it is the responsibility of the supervisor to help the supervisee with work-related problems, concern with accountability, control, direction—the administrative component of supervision—is an ubiquitous element providing an additional focus of attention. Thus, unlike supervision, consultation is more often time-limited, goal-limited, situationally focused, segmented problem-oriented.

However, the distinctive difference most frequently cited in distinguishing between these two indirect services is that the consultee-consultant relationship, unlike the supervisory relationship, is a voluntary one, taking place outside the hierarchical administrative channels. The consultant has, therefore, no positional authority with regard to the supervisee. Consequently, the consultee is free to accept or reject, modify, adapt, and so forth, the outcome of the consultation process. It offers "the freedom to seek assistance without granting authority to those who give assistance." It makes available "help without control," without the need to adhere to the consultant's advice, suggestion, or recommendations and without the requirement that the consultee be accountable to the consultant. The consultee remains the determinant of his actions without any dilution of his rights and responsibilities as a consequence of his acceptance of consultation. The reason the consultee is free of accountability to the consultant is because he is accountable elsewhere. The consultee is accountable for the use of the consultation to his own supervisor. He is not, then, entirely free of constraints in the use he makes of the consultation.

The kind of authority exercised in supervision as contrasted with that available to the consultant is delineated by Simon (1965) when he says:

> The characteristic which distinguishes authority from other kinds of influence is this—the subordinate holds in abeyance his own critical faculties for choosing between alternatives and uses the formal criterion of the receipt of a command or a signal as his basis for choice. On the other hand a person who receives a suggestion (as in consultation) accepts it as only one of the evidential bases for making his choice, but the choice he will make depends upon conviction. (pp. 126–27)

And yet, perhaps the distinction which is so frequently cited is not as incontestable as one would like. The widely accepted suggestion that the relationship between supervisee and supervisor changes gradually to that of consultee and consultant implies that supervisors can, while in their position, relate differently to the worker. It would suggest that at some point the supervisor can set aside administrative authority and discuss a work-related problem with the supervisee, now in the role of consultee, without any complication of continual worker accountability. This is predicated on the supposition that the supervisor can be a consultant while still a supervisor.

There are further difficulties with the distinction made between supervision and consultation from the consultant's side of the desk. While the consultant has no formal administrative authority, he is not entirely free from authority. If the consultant comes into the agency at the request of the administration, if the agency makes available consultation at agency expense, even though the consultant is without explicit authority, nevertheless the consultee might recognize that he will be held accountable for the consequences of the consultation. The tendency is to see the consultant as associated with the administration and carrying some of the administrative authority that relates to the administration hierarchy.

When the agency administration sanctions and encourages the use of consultation, takes the trouble to make it available, and goes to the expense of financing it, rejection of consultation is difficult:

> Under such circumstances the consultant is symbolic of the administration which retained him and which he represents and has attributed to him some of its authority. . . . Rejection of the [consultant's suggestions] may be interpreted as running counter to administrative wishes. In such a position the consultant carries with him the aura of delegated decision making from the administration. (Gaupp, 1966, p. 208)

Even if the only source of influence which the consultant brings into the relationship is that of the "power of his expertise" this does not leave the consultee entirely free. The constraints, while attitudinal, are nevertheless real. To reject the suggestions of an "expert" indicates that the

wisdom, experience, and prestige of the consultant are being chal-
lenged as well as the cumulative judgments of all those who have
previously given to him his special prestige. . . . Consultees who
are faced with a high status representative from another profession
about which they have little knowledge seem to see the alternatives
as either accepting the consultant's recommendations and insights or
facing the mystical disapproval of the entire alien profession. (Gaupp,
1966, p. 209)

Rejection also imposes on the consultee full responsibility for a
course of action disapproved of by some one who is recognized
as having more expert knowledge about the problem.

The consultant is not neutral in his attitude toward the advice and suggestion he might offer. If he has a conviction in the
utility of his recommendations for improved service and if he is
concerned that the client be given the best possible service, he
would be concerned about the rejection of his recommendations
and overtly, or covertly, press for the implementation of his recommendations. Once again, the consultee is not entirely free of
constraints in making a decision on the use of consultation.

Social work consultation is sometimes given, or received, in
circumstances which imply a condition of administrative controls
not altogether unlike those encountered in supervision. For example, state departments of public welfare make available consultation by specialists in adoption, foster care, institutional care,
and so on, to community agencies planning such programs. At
the same time, the state departments have the responsibility for
licensing the agencies to perform such functions and offer such
services. The power to license, or to refuse to license, by the
agency that the consultants represent gives the consultant some
positional administrative authority, even though the consultant
may reject or deny it.

Consultants in federal and state departments who offer consultation to local or county social agencies often have implied administrative functions, are responsible to the community for the

level of service offered by the consulting agency, and consequently are concerned with the results of their consultation. Similarly, state licensing units that have the responsibility for consultation, for instance with day care centers, find it difficult to maintain the fiction that day care personnel are free to accept or reject their suggestions. The fact that they do represent the licensing authority belies this contention. "Rejection of the content of the consultation implies rejection of the standards of the agency which has legal controls" (Gaupp, 1966, p. 207).

The program director of a public health agency evaluation unit notes that "as I wear two hats, administrator and consultant, confusion is inevitable and occasionally a recommendation is perceived as a mandate."

The extreme contingency is cited by Kiester (1969). Suppose in the course of consultation "situations came to the attention of the consultant which are so damaging to [clients] and so unresponsive to the offer of consultative help that action to protect the client is indicated." Kiester says, in raising the question about day care centers, that in such instances "referral should be made to the persons or agency responsible for legal action to discontinue the operation of the facility" (p. 8). While this is, admittedly, the extreme instance, it reflects a pressure felt by consultees receiving consultation from licensing agencies.

Consultation is often regarded as a component of the regulatory responsibilities of licensing agencies. As part of its program review functions the agency offers consultation for the purpose of helping the consultee agency to improve its services beyond compliance with minimum standards of care (Polenz, 1970).

The same problem is encountered by the consultee when he faces a consultant from any standard-setting agency whose support for confirmation the consultee's agency might need. These include agencies such as the Child Welfare League of America, the Council on Social Work Education, and the Family Service Association of America. For instance, consultants representing the Council on Social Work Education made over two hundred site visits in 1973, met with social work educators for consultation sessions at the office of the Council, and answered numerous letters and phone calls requesting help. The consultants provided help on the basis of their specialized knowledge regarding social work curriculum, faculty requirements, school organization and administration, student admission, development of, and planning for, new schools and departments of social work, and so on. Their specialized knowledge and experience regarding the problems relating to social work education faced by the consultees enabled them successfully to implement their role as consultants. However, the Council accredits programs on both graduate and undergraduate levels. Council accreditation is required in order for the school to be eligible for student and faculty stipends, and only graduates of accredited schools are eligible for some social work positions. Consultation, consequently, implies some clear constraints about the advisability of accepting the recommendations of such consultants.

A similar problem is encountered by consultants who represent fund-granting agencies—the Office of Child Development, the National Institutes of Health, the Office of Economic Opportunity, local community welfare councils.

Caplan (1970) recognizes the general problem that while consultation is clearly distinguished from supervision in the administrative hierarchical sense, it is, nevertheless, replete with hierarchical elements. He notes that "it is hard for the staff to see the consultant as having only the authority of ideas and it is hard for the [consultant] to divest himself from the mantle of power handed over to him by the director as well as invested in him by the social evaluation of his professional status" (p. 273).

A further, related, distinction is made between supervision and consultation on the basis of the worker's freedom of choice. However, while it is clear that the supervisory relationship is not voluntary but rather a requirement of the agency, it is not always true that the use of consultation is entirely voluntary.

There are various degrees of voluntarism. Often workers use consultation because it is expected of them, because it has been "suggested" by the supervisor, as a consequence of professional peer pressure, and so forth.

While these provisos weaken the distinctions between supervision and consultation they do not nullify them. It is still true that consultation is a staff assignment and supervision a line position in the administrative hierarchy. While psychological and attitudinal considerations make consultation less voluntary and more authoritative than is generally thought to be the case, the consultee is freer than the supervisee in deciding on asking for, and using the results of, consultation as compared with supervision. This is the conclusion reached by Lounsberry and Hall (1976) who confirm Polenz's (1970) general finding that licensing supervision (the mandatory monitoring and enforcing of compliance with standards) and licensing consultation (the voluntary solicitation of help from the licensing agent in program improvement) are not necessarily antithetical functions. They found that in the majority of state programs, "consultation is part of the official role of the day care licensing staff" (p. 516). However,

> In interviews with twenty licensed day care homes and center directors, researchers were told that licensers had in no way attempted to use their regulatory power to influence acceptance of consultation advice. The main reservation which licensees expressed toward licensers offering consultation was that, in their opinion, the licenser was often not adequately trained in matters such as child development, to offer constructive recommendations. (p. 518)

While these factors are characteristic of consultation they are not uniquely distinctive. The worker is in contact with many people in the agency and in the professional community who have no administrative authority over him and with whom he might voluntarily choose to discuss professional matters. This makes these people confidants but does not as yet make them consultants. The one indispensable, uniquely differentiating attribute of a consultant is that he possesses some expert knowledge and/or skill relevant to the problem the prospective consultee faces which is not otherwise available. The prospective consultee needs this expertise in dealing with his problem, and when he decides to make use of the consultant's expertise he accepts the status of consultee. This, then, is ultimately what truly distinguishes the consultant from the supervisor—the possession of some special knowledge and skill different from, or beyond that, possessed by the supervisor.

One might say that the consultant begins where the supervisor ends. There may be some situations which are problematic for the supervisee with which the supervisor cannot help, either because they require some specialized knowledge, or because they require a higher level of skill with regard to the kind of knowledge he holds, which is beyond the supervisor. The consultant who has the specialized knowledge, or the higher level of expertise, is then brought in and offers the help of this special knowledge to the consultee. The consultant is distinguished from the supervisor in that he has either a higher level of knowledge of the same kinds of content with which the supervisor is concerned, or a specialized kind of knowledge and skill which the supervisor is not expected to have.

The problem the supervisee faces is thus either outside the scope of the supervisor's knowledge or beyond the depth of the supervisor's knowledge. "The consultant, therefore, is a resource person called upon to provide that 'something' which the supervisor and local staff cannot provide. He is a specialist in a certain field" (Rieman, 1963, p. 85). Consultation might be regarded as an adjunctive function to supervision or a supplementation of supervision.

The rationale for psychiatric case consultation in a public

child welfare agency clearly spells this out. Supervisors reporting on their experience with consultation in such an agency note
that:

> Consultation is requested on a case when the case worker and his
> supervisor together need the consultant's help in clarifying and eval-
> uating their assessment of the psychological problem with which the
> client is faced as he attempts to deal with his social situation. Thus a
> case is selected for consultation when the caseworker and the super-
> visor together want to increase their understanding of the psycholo-
> gical aspects of an individual or family situation or when the in-
> terplay between psychological, somatic and environmental factors in
> the client's problem is obscure. (Cohen, Abma, and Selterman,
> 1972, p. 13)

In reporting on the use of a casework consultant in a camp
setting, Berg (1959) points to this difference between the respective responsibilities of supervisor and consultant. The camp
"counselors were supervised directly by a unit leader. . . .
When the counselor needed help with problems with which the
unit leader supervisor did not feel he was expert enough to assist
. . . the consultant worked with the unit leader on the problem
and the unit leader (supervisor) then attempted to help the
counselor with it." In other instances, the limits of the supervisor's expertise having been reached, "the consultant worked
directly with the counselor" on the work problem he faced (p.
410). This clearly points to the limits of supervisory expertise as
the criteria for a consultation request and distinguishes between
the responsibilities of supervision and consultation.

One of the earlier articles reporting on the use of consultants in social agencies points to this distinction. Drake (1946)
states that justification for the use of the consultant lies in the
fact that the "consultant is presumed to be more expert in certain prescribed areas than administrative or supervisory personnel can reasonably be expected to become" (p. 88).

A psychiatrist detailing his experience as a consultant to the Los Angeles Bureau of Public Assistance notes that

> when a caseworker has difficulties with a client, he will, as a rule, first turn to his supervisor for some help. In many instances the problem can be resolved because of the supervisor's greater technical and professional experience. When, however, both caseworker and supervisor have reached their limit or when the supervisor feels that the difficulties are related to some personality problem in the caseworker then they will request a mental health consultation. (Rogawski, 1968, p. 76)

The same difference between supervisor and consultant is noted in nursing consultation: "A consultant can be used effectively when the supervisor and her staff have exhausted their own resources. . . . A hospital had been given new equipment for a nursery for premature infants and the nurses and their supervisors did not know how to use it so the nursing director called in a pediatric nursing consultant" (Rumrill, 1957, p. 165).

Generally, the expertise which the consultant provides is not one that the consultee has a professional responsibility to acquire since it is not central to his primary tasks. If the information and skill were a regular, essential component of the activity the professional routinely performs it would become part of the formal agenda for training the professional and, ultimately, the consultants would not be needed. The social worker consulting the psychiatrist about anticonvulsive drugs for an epileptic, the social work administrator consulting an accountant about fiscal procedures, an adoption worker consulting a lawyer about the legalities of international adoption are all concerned with soliciting information which is not part of their professional preparation and only occasionally needed.

Supervision is invariably done by a professional who has a professional affiliation similar to that of the supervisee. The consultant, on the other hand, is frequently, although not invariably, affiliated with a profession which is different from that of the consultee. The consultation provides expertise which is not readily available through supervision within the organization. A United Nations study on consultation notes this distinctive aspect of consultation. Bringing an expert into the organization from outside on a temporary contractual basis is, they say, an efficient procedure for meeting organizational needs. "Consultants provide a ready source of skills, knowledge or expertise which are not readily available to the client organization." This permits help "with some kinds of problems which are not frequent enough to warrant the use of permanent staff having the necessary ability" to deal with these problems (United Nations, 1968, p. 2).

Thorne (1975) points out that "many agencies which could not afford to maintain a technical specialist on their payroll will call in a consultant for special information or analyses. Thus, consultation is an economical means to increase the technical competence of an organization" (p. 359).

If the agency's need for the specialized knowledge is sufficiently recurrent, the specialist's function may be incorporated into the agency structure as a regular staff position. Thus, public welfare agencies have staff positions for nutritionists, home economists, lawyers, and psychologists. Such specialists, as members of the agency staff, may, in addition to performing their own functions, offer consultation to other staff members regarding problems relevant to the consultant's special knowledge and training. Even though this makes consultation available in-house, the consultant staff member provides a kind of help which the consultee's supervisor is not expected to be able to provide. While consultation occurs between people who are equal in different areas of expertise, supervision occurs between people who have different levels of expertise within the same area.

STAFF DEVELOPMENT AND IN-SERVICE TRAINING

It seems difficult to distinguish much consultant activity from staff development or in-service training (for instance, see Altrocchi, Spielberger, and Eisdorfer, 1965; Tobiessen and Shai, 1971). A distinction might be made on the basis of the fact that in-service education is formal and organized, and has a general predetermined content which all need to learn but which is not of particular direct relevance to the individual work problem of any one worker. As against the orderly, systematic coverage of content in an in-service training program the teaching-learning content of consultation is determined by problems the consultee brings. Consultation more frequently is concerned with specific work problems encountered by a worker or group of workers, and sessions are not scheduled according to some course outline but on an *ad hoc,* impromptu, opportunistic basis as particular problems arise. In-service training is concerned with problems which might be encountered; consultation is concerned with problems that have actually been encountered. In-service training is preparatory effort to prevent work problems from arising; consultation is remediation for problems which have arisen.

Unlike the in-service trainer,

> the consultant does not have responsibility for instruction on all aspects of the consultee's job but only for those aspects which are related to the problem with which the consultee wants help. The emphasis in in-service training is on principles and techniques; the emphasis in consultation is on helping the consultee find a workable solution for the specific problem under consideration. (Insley, 1959, p. 217)

Consultation offers deliberately "selected professional learning for use in appropriate situations" (Rosenthal and Sullivan, 1959, p. 6).

The content of consultation is the consultee's individual work; the content of in-service training is general material of relevance to, but not directly focused on, the consultee's own work. The focus of in-service training is on learning first with the anticipation that it will be applicable to problem-solving in the future. The focus of consultation is on problem-solving first in the hope that the consultee will learn some generalization that will be applicable in the future. The focus of in-service training is on the general learning needs of many; the focus of consultation is on the specific "opportunistic," immediate learning needs of the individual consultee regarding problems encountered with a particular client under particular conditions. In-service training is predisposed to the establishment of a didactic pupil/teacher relationship; consultation depends on a more coordinate collaborative relationship.

THERAPY

There are significant aspects of similarity between consultation and all forms of therapy so that some confusion is almost inevitable. In both processes someone has a problem and needs help and someone is cast in the role of the helper. In both, essentially similar procedures are used in implementing the process of helping in the context of a relationship characterized by similar facilitative conditions.

In fact, some of the more general definitions of consultation are equally applicable to the casework, counseling, therapy processes. Defining consultation as "the giving and taking of help in an interpersonal relationship" (Wolfe, 1966, p. 132) or stating, as does Lippitt (1959), that "consultation, like love . . . is a general label for many varieties of relationships between a professional helper (consultant) and a help needing system consultee" (p. 5), makes it difficult to distinguish between consultation and therapy.

There are, however, some clear distinctions between therapy and consultation. They relate principally to the focus and intent of the consultant's interventions. The problems of concern in therapy are personal problems which may or may not be job-related. The focus of consultation is exclusively and deliberately concerned only with those problems that are clearly job-related. All of the client's significant social roles may be grist for the therapy mill, only one clearly defined social role—the occupational role—is the legitimate concern of consultation. The question the consultant asks of the consultee is "How can I help you in your work?" The question the therapist asks of the client is: "How can I help you?" Only as the consultee's behavior, attitudes, and feelings are manifested in some on-the-job dysfunctioning do these become matters of possible consultation intervention.

The intent of therapy is to help the client become a better adjusted person generally so that she or he can deal more effectively with life problems. The intent of the consultant is not to help the client become a more effective person, but rather to help the client become only a more effective worker. The intent is to effect changes in the consultee's professional identity and attitudes, not in his personal identity and attitudes.

In implementing these distinctions between consultation and therapy, the consultant keeps the discussion focused on job-related considerations. Discussion of the worker's attitudes, feelings, and behavior is introduced only by indirection, in terms of their derivatives as related to the consultee's professional activity in relation to their clients. By keeping the focus of the consultation "out there," the consultant hopes to deal with the worker's personal problems, as reflected in job performance, only through indirection and metaphor.

These distinctions which are easily drawn on paper are admittedly much more difficult to follow in the living consultative interaction. This is particularly true of one kind of consultation—consultee-centered consultation which is primarily concerned with the attitudinal and behavioral contribution which the consultee makes to the work problems he is facing. But articulated distinctions which are difficult to apply are somewhat better than no distinctions at all.

COLLABORATION

A further distinction might be made between consultation and collaboration. Collaboration involves the joint working together, as a team, in response to a problem with which the client wants help. Both collaborating professionals bring their specialized, differentiated expertise and competence to bear in helping the client in his situation. The efforts of one professional complement and supplement the efforts of the other. It is a relationship in which the collaborators work side by side. Consultation, on the other hand, is directed toward maximizing the effectiveness of the expertise and competence of one of the professionals involved in working with the client—the consultee. Collaborators have equal responsibility for case outcome. In consultation the consultee has primary responsibility for the implementation of the necessary interventions.

Summary

A review was presented of some of the distinctive aspects of consultation as evidenced by the general definitions of consultation. A distinctive definition of social work consultation was then suggested. Differences between social work consultation and other similar processes such as supervision, in-service training, therapy and collaboration were identified.

Chapter Three

Social Workers
as Consultees
and Consultants

In chapter 1 we reviewed some of the earlier literature on the experience of social workers with consultation in which social workers were most frequently cast in the role of consultees. The consultant in the majority of instances was a psychiatrist employed by the social agency part time.

Statistics collected by the Family Service Association of America from member agencies indicate that this general situation is still prevalent. In January, 1975, family service agencies employed a total of 314 consultants from fields other than social work. By far the largest percentage of such consultants, some 55 percent, were psychiatrists. Psychologists and lawyers were among the other kinds of professionals employed as consultants to agency personnel (Family Service Association of America 1975).

There has been a downward trend in the employment of consultants from other fields by family service agencies since 1963. Family service agencies may not be representative, however, and the trend may be more in response to fiscal stringency than to changing patterns of need. In any case, 19 percent fewer consultants from fields outside social work were employed by family service agencies in January, 1976, as compared with January, 1975.

In Chapter I we noted that a recent study of child care service-delivery systems indicated a growing need for lawyers as consultants. This is understandable in view of the many legal questions regarding child protection, custody, and guardianship with which such agencies are concerned.

Bell (1975) notes that:

> Providing legal consultation to [child welfare] workers is a means of imparting legal information which would assist [them] in securing permanency or protecting the child, particularly when arduous legal proceedings may be involved. Expanding legal knowledge adds to the repertoire of techniques available to social workers in their efforts to accomplish efficiently as possible restoration, reliquishments, terminations, and successful long term foster care. . . .
> Legal consultation can be utilized for both staff training and care consultation. (p. 33)

In one instance a state department of children and family services instituted a legal consultation program by "employing an attorney of family law on an hourly basis to consult with a staff of thirty child welfare workers" (Bell 1975, p. 37). The consultant helped the workers to understand state statutes governing child welfare, clarified rules of evidence, developed a greater awareness of what was expected in preparing a case for court.

Bell (1976) details the variety of contributions that medical consultants can make to the services provided by child welfare agencies. Knowledge about the medical situation of their clients is an important concern of child welfare workers, and medical consultants can be of help in medical diagnostic evaluation, treatment planning, and medical resource location and utilization. Significant decisions in planning for a child for whom the agency has responsibility frequently involve medical evaluations of the child, thus requiring medical consultation.

The Child Welfare League of America statement of standards for services such as foster family care, adoptions, institutional care, protective services, and services to unmarried parents spells out the contributions which medical, psychiatric, psychological, and legal consultants can make to the ongoing services of the agency (see, for instance, Child Welfare League of America, 1975, pp. 88–89).

In addition to receiving consultation from psychiatrists, lawyers, and psychologists, social workers also seek consultation from doctors (other than psychiatrists), nutritionists, occupational therapists, and home economists.

More recently, social workers and social work agencies have sought consultation from a variety of experts with whom they previously had little or no contact. Computer programmers have consulted with social workers concerning computerization of agency operations; business management consultants have helped in the reorganization of public welfare systems and large voluntary agencies; organizational analysts have, through consultation, introduced social agency personnel to such procedures as management by objectives, synectics or brainstorming, computer simulation, problem census, delphi and nominal group decision-making, functional job analysis, and program evaluation and review.

Since social work purports to be concerned with the "whole client" and supposedly takes some responsibility for dealing with a wide range of problems, consultation from specialists would seem to be almost mandatory. No social worker can adequately possess the knowledge required to understand and offer help to the "whole client." His knowledge needs to be supplemented by the expertise of professionals in many areas.

In addition, consultants may be used to provide effective liaison between the social agency and some professional groups with which the agency has to work. Thus medical consultants are needed by public welfare agencies in negotiating with local medical groups about medical services provided for their clients.

Social workers also receive consultation from other social workers who have some specialized expertise. The 1975 Family Service Association of America report cited above noted that nationwide member agencies employed thirty-six people with the title of social work consultant.

By far, most of the literature relating to social workers as consultees reports them as seeking help from psychiatrists in case consultation to further their understanding of the psychodynamics of client behavior. Psychiatrists also provide help in formulating treatment programs and in making differential diagnoses of suspected psychotic clients. The consulting help sought by social workers is, however, much more varied than is suggested by the literature.

In trying to define the circumstances which lead social workers to request consultation we asked participants in three different institutes on social work consultation—some fifty-five workers—to engage in the following exercise: "Describe briefly the situation when you hollered (or were tempted to holler): Is there a consultant in the house?"

Analysis of the responses indicates that the key consideration was a problem that had been encountered on the job, the solution to which appeared to be beyond the capacity of the worker and his immediate supervisor. Often consultation was required because the needed specialized knowledge and/or specialized competence resided in a profession other than social work.

Workers said:

> When I was working with a family who had a severely retarded child, the parents asked me questions about seizure control. I had some ideas but was hesitant about sounding off until I had some medical consultation on this.

My client was an acting-out adolescent male who was a trial to his family, the school, the neighborhood, to himself—and to me. Nevertheless, he had considerable potential and the backing of the agency in working with him. We had tried every approach that I or the supervisor could dream up and nothing worked—at least not very well. We decided to get psychiatric consultation.

My supervisor and I agreed we could both productively use consultation in making a decision on an adoptive placement with which we had been struggling for months. The adoptive mother had a mental breakdown about 8 years ago shortly after her marriage but seems to have fully recovered. Yet there was enough concern about the stability of her current functioning so that she seemed somewhat of a risk. In all other respects the placement seemed a good home for the child we had in mind. We asked for a psychiatric consultation on this primarily, I think, to confirm our own decision and, I guess, to share the burden of responsibility for the decision. It was a move designed to give us the emotional support we needed to move on this.

I handled a difficult case that involved the adoption of a Korean child. At one point the legal aspects of the case needed clarification to protect the rights of the prospective adoptive couple and to ensure the preservation of the home for the child. At this point I requested, and obtained, legal consultation.

Another worker and myself, with the approval of the agency, were interested in doing a research project on the effectiveness of our casework with senior citizens. We knew little about questionnaire construction, less about sampling procedures, and least about statistical procedures. We asked for consultation from the faculty member who taught courses in social work research at the University School of Social Work.

Working with an unmarried mother who was interested in finding out about and using some contraceptive procedure. I had a good relationship with her and she herself was reluctant to discuss this with a doctor. I consulted with a gynecologist to get more details on contraceptive procedures which my client could consider.

I was working with a couple who had marital problems. Child care for their year-old son was a matter of concern since he was somewhat retarded and husband and wife had conflicts as to what might be best for him. They were considering a day care center placement for him, but the mother was ambivalent because she was not sure that the child could meet the demands of such a setting. At one point in our contact they asked for an assessment of the child's learning capabilities. They wanted to know exactly what tests were available to clarify this. Since the information requested required a knowledge of psychometrics I consulted with a psychologist.

I was involved in setting up the procedure for admitting children to a detention home. This was a new program for the agency and nobody knew much about this. I was assigned to visit other detention homes and consult with the people who had experience in administering such a facility.

As a school social worker I had contact with a hyperactive child who was very disturbing to the teacher and the class. In working with the teacher on this we both agreed that it might be useful to try a behavioral modification procedure. Since my supervisor had little experience with such an approach, arrangements were made for consultation with a psychologist who was experienced in behavioral modification.

The agency decided to develop and maintain a community-based group treatment facility for children. We felt a need for consultation from social service consultants from the state in finding out how to go about doing something like this.

It happened when we were trying to comply with the directives to separate social services from income maintenance. I had a difficult caseload and the supervisor was just as confused, if not more confused, than I was. I did get some help from a state consultant who knew more about this than anybody else.

I was working in a teen-age drop-in center in a white middle-class neighborhood when one of the older adolescents requested an interview with me. He told me he had been taking heroin and was now seriously interested in the methadone program. He wanted to know what was involved and how to get into it. Since I had no previous experience or orientation in drug abuse I consulted with the social worker assigned to a local methadone program.

One worker wrote facetiously but nevertheless answered to the point:

I hollered for a consultant when I started to go about tanning a raccoon pelt to make it into a raccoon hat. I knew nothing about doing this but wanted to learn since I had the raccoon pelt and the material from the library book was difficult to understand. I wanted someone to help me, to answer my questions but not to do it for me.

Social Workers as Consultants

THE CONSULTEES TO WHOM SOCIAL WORK CONSULTATION IS OFFERED

Social work consultants operate in the area of interdisciplinary collaborative contact with other professionals, particularly in host settings. School social workers consult with teachers and school administrators; medical social workers consult with doctors and nurses in hospital settings; psychiatric social workers consult with psychiatrists, psychologists, and nurses in mental institutions and in community mental health agencies; community workers consult with a variety of different professionals in urban-renewal programs. Such consultation involves a social worker and a member of another profession.

Social workers also act as consultants to other social workers. They act as consultants in helping social workers develop new services requiring the specialized knowledge of the consultant—half-way houses, day care centers, homemaker services, senior citizen programs, foster grandparents program, and so forth.

We have mentioned the employment of social workers as consultants by national standard-setting agencies and by governmental agencies offering a consultative program relating to licensing of child welfare services. Medical social workers are employed as consultants in the crippled children programs; social work researchers are employed as consultants on social work research projects. Medical social work consultation (Simon, 1966) and psychiatric social work consultation (May, 1970) have been offered to public assistance workers in county welfare departments and to child welfare workers (Rosenthal and Sullivan, 1959).

For a time, provisions of the Social Security Act relating to Medicare required that nursing homes serving Medicare patients have social work consultation. This provided consultation assignments for many social workers with medical, geriatric, and institutional care specializations.

The recent development and proliferation of client organizations have resulted in requests for social work consultation. Organizations of foster parents and adoptive parents have used social workers as consultants. An organization of abusive parents—Parents Anonymous—was organized in consultation with a protective service social worker. Social workers have consulted with groups of parents of retarded children who were interested in organizing for the purpose of obtaining special education programs for their children. A recent report by Collins and Pancoast (1976) details the work of social work consultants in working with neighborhood groups of family day care workers.

With the increasing use by caseworkers of other modalities such as group and community organization approaches, both group workers and community organizers have recently, and increasingly, offered consultation to casework agencies. With increasing use of paraprofessionals in a variety of human services facilities such as Head Start and homemaker home–health aid services social workers have been called on to offer consultation to such groups of workers.

We noted that federal legislation with regard to mental health centers required consultation as one of the services made available to the community. As a consequence, many psychiatric social workers employed by mental health centers are providing consultation to other social workers, to court and correctional personnel, to schools, churches, and community groups.

Frequently, consultation is a component of the social worker's ongoing job responsibilities without being explicitly identified as such. Social workers in host settings, working on interdisciplinary teams or in collaborative activities with other professionals, are constantly involved in consultation. They answer questions about social work resources; they provide input on the social components of case situations in helping other professionals understand these aspects of the problem; they contribute their expertise regarding the social antecedents, concomitants, and consequences of the clients' problematic situation in hospitals, old age homes, schools, and court settings.

The social work consultants in nursing homes are consulted about problems relating to adjustment to the nursing home on the part of the resident and his family; reactions to death and dying; motivation of residents to become involved in group activities; activity programs for depressed, isolated, withdrawn residents; the effective use of volunteers; formulation of psychosocially defensible visiting hours procedures, and more effective communication patterns across different shifts (Austin and Kosberg, 1976).

Social workers offer consultation to parents in family service agencies and child guidance units of mental health centers in offering an indirect service to children. The parents-consultees are provided with the orientation skills and know-how which enable them to act as change agents for their children (Reisinger, Ora, and Frangia, 1976).

Social workers offer consultation to the foster parents of children for whom they have responsibility, as part of their ongoing relationship with the foster family. They offer consultation to prospective adoptive parents regarding the decision to adopt, and to adoptive parents after placement regarding problems of the child's adjustment to adoption and desirable procedures for telling the child about adoption. Social workers offer consultation to homemaker-home health aids in the child welfare and geriatric services.

In attempting to determine more systematically the professional designation and the organizational affiliation of those to whom social workers offer consultation, questionnaires were mailed in 1976 to the 970 members of the National Association of Social Workers who had identified their primary job responsibility as that of consultation. Four hundred and eighty-three usable responses were received, a respectable response rate. The study will be referred to in the text as the Kadushin-Buckman survey (1977).

Respondents had considerable social work education and experience, some 95 percent having either an M.S.W. or a more advanced degree and an average of fifteen years of paid experience in social work. They had an average of ten years of experience as consultants.

As might be expected, given the level of experience, the group is older than the general NASW membership. Group mean age is forty-seven years. However, the sex distribution of the respondent group is very similar to that of NASW membership generally—64 percent female, 36 percent male.

The largest single group of respondents (25.6 percent) was affiliated with a psychiatric-mental health agency. Other large clusters of respondents were affiliated with a child welfare or family service agency (18 percent) or with school social work units (17.6 percent). Some 7 percent of the respondents were in private practice, and the group included some retired social workers.

The questionnaire presented a list of different professional groups and different community organizations and requested that the respondent note the frequency with which he or she offered consultation to each of the professionals and each of the organizations.

Social work consultants most frequently acted as consultants to other social workers. Consultation to both nurses and teachers was common but still considerably less than the frequency with which social workers saw other social workers as consultees. Consultation with doctors and psychologists was provided in almost equal modest frequency, but lawyers, judges, police, and clergymen were relatively rarely seen as consultees. Table 1 lists the frequency with which professionally designated groups were identified as consultees by the respondents.

Consultants listed less frequent contact with a wide variety of other kinds of personnel. The scatter included recreational workers, rehabilitation workers, occupational therapists, voca-

Table 1 Frequency of Consultation with Designated Professionals During Past Year, in Percent

$(N = 478)$

Consultees' Professional Designation	Frequency		
	Frequently	Occasionally	Rarely or Never
Social workers	35.2	13.2	2.0
Nurses	15.6	15.6	7.0
Teachers	15.1	12.5	9.0
Psychologists	10.0	13.7	10.0
Doctors	12.0	13.7	10.0
Clergymen	4.0	11.6	13.0
Lawyers	3.0	7.6	16.0
Police	3.0	7.6	15.0
Judges	2.0	4.5	17.0
Total	100.0	100.0	100.0

tional counselors, housing specialists, community planners, nutritionists, case aids and volunteers, agency board members, and legislators.

While the data available do not provide any explanation for the concentration of social work consultation efforts with other social workers, we might speculate that other professionals do not have a clear idea of the kinds of expertise which a social work consultant might possess. The ambiguity of the professional image may make it difficult for professionals other than social workers to recognize that a social work consultant can contribute to the solution of professional problems encountered by other professionals. Accessibility may also be a factor. Social work consultants who work in the same social agency with other social workers may be, consequently, more accessible for consultation. This concentration of social work consultation efforts with social workers as consultees is noted by other researchers, and similar as well as additional hypotheses are advanced in explaining this.

A study of social work consultation in programs for children indicated that, most often, social workers as consultants provided consultation to other social workers. As consultees, social workers received consultation most frequently from psychiatrists (McClung, and Stunden, 1972, p. 35). The fact that most often the recipient of social work consultation is another social worker is quite different from the pattern which typifies other mental health center professionals. The more frequent pattern is that of a consultant from one profession giving consultation to a consultee from another profession. It is attributable in part to "the absence of a formal body of knowledge unique to the profession of social work" (p. 33) and the lack of a clearly identifiable, unique, differentiating expertise.

Another explanation lies in status differences. Given the relative prestige of the different professions which are related to each other in a manner which might result in consultative relationship, the pattern noted above of social work consultation to social work consultee is to be anticipated. A study of the relationship between collaborating professionals noted that

> when a person provides advice for others he is usually in a position which implies that he is superior and that the consultees are dependent upon him. . . . The prescribed relations among these roles would have psychiatrists seldom turning to members of the ancillary professions for consultation. Similarly the adjunct groups would anticipate only infrequent solicitation of their advice by a superior. Our data indicate that the prescription holds true. A majority of the psychiatrists state that they gave advice more than they asked for it. Only one-fifth of the social workers and psychologists state that psychiatrists seek their advice. (Zander, Cohen and Stotland, 1966, p. 241)

The professional designation of the most frequently seen consultee is reflected further in the agencies to which the consultants most frequently offer service (Table 2). These include health service agencies, mental health and child care agencies, and school and family service agencies. Less frequently, consultation is given to criminal justice agencies or to church organizations. An interesting finding, not apparent from the request for specification of the professional affiliation of the consultee, is that social workers frequently proffer consultation to lay people involved in social welfare activities through citizens and parents groups.

SITUATIONS REQUIRING SOCIAL WORK CONSULTATION

An institute exercise similar to the one described above concerning social work consultees, but this time focused on social work consultants, provided information about the activities of social work consultants. Social work consultants were called in to help "establish an effective foster home recruitment program"; "to establish a day care center in a low-income neighborhood"; "to help clarify procedures for Medicare and medical reimbur-

Table 2 Frequency with Which Consultation Was Offered to Designated Agencies During Past Year, in Percent

(N = 472)

Consultee Agencies or Organizations	Frequency		
	Frequently	Occasionally	Rarely or Never
Health service agencies	14.3	10.0	6.3
Schools	13.5	9.0	8.0
Mental health agencies	11.6	11.3	6.7
Child care agencies	11.6	10.0	8.0
Family service agencies	7.5	11.0	9.0
Nursing homes	7.7	5.0	12.0
Rehabilitation agencies	7.3	10.0	9.0
Criminal justice agencies	4.7	7.0	12.0
Churches	3.7	7.0	12.0
Parents or parent groups	11.0	9.4	7.7
Citizen groups	8.0	10.0	9.0
Total	100.0	100.0	100.0

sement"; "to discuss the need for procedures, mechanics, curriculum of an in-service training program for protective service workers"; "to consult with teachers regarding community resources for emotionally disturbed pupils"; "to work with doctors and parents regarding the crippled children's program"; "to help foster parents organize a foster parents association"; "to assist in organizing a medical social work unit in a newly established medical facility."

Social workers as consultants say: "I consulted with the president of a neighborhood house board in helping her with procedures for negotiating funding from the local welfare council"; "I consulted with the officials of the Head Start program in formulating a program to provide knowledge about, and actuate interest in, the local Head Start program. The program was directed to low-income residents of the community."

In attempting to learn in greater detail the situations in which social workers are called on to act as consultants, the

Kadushin-Buckman survey requested the following information from respondents:

Think back over your most recent typical consultation assignment. Very briefly state: (1) the professional designation of the consultee; (2) the setting to which you were a consultant; (3) the problem that required your consultation.

Types of Consultation

We have organized the responses in terms of types of consultation provided by social workers. A variety of schemes has been proposed for organizing the various types of consultation. McClung and Stunden (1972) list seven discrete types of consultation, Caplan (1970), four; Haylett and Rapoport (1964), three; MacLennan, Quinn, and Schroeder (1971), two. We have selected the rubric formulated by Caplan (1970) in organizing the responses to the questionnaire request. This listing is frequently used in the consultation literature; it seems reasonably comprehensive and, at the same time, not unneccessarily detailed. The four categories proposed, which relate to the central focus and indicate the target of consultation, follow. It might be well to note that the categories are not neatly demarcated and there is often some overlap encountered in the realities of practice. Note, too, that I have taken some liberties paraphrasing Caplan which may result in some slight alterations of his typology.

1. *Client-centered case consultation.* The content of the consultation is work-difficulty related to a particular client or a group of clients. "The consultant helps by bringing his specialized knowledge and skills to bear in making an expert assessment of the nature of the client's problem and in recommending how the con-

sultee should deal with the case. The primary goal of the consultation is for the consultant to communicate to the consultee how this client can be helped" (Caplan, 1970, p. 32). The target of change is the client. The client may be an individual, group, or community.

The teacher consultee may want help in knowing how to deal with the disruptive behavior of a child in class; a nurse consultee may need information on nursing home facilities in the community for a geriatric patient; a social work consultee may need assistance in helping a client qualify for subsidized education; a worker uses consultation to understand more fully and help more adequately a child manifesting separation anxiety; a group work consultant consults with a worker responsible for a parent group in a family counseling program regarding special behavioral modification procedures which might be employed in a group context; a consultant representing the National Welfare Rights organization helps a community organizer with problems in activating a local unit.

> The primary purpose of [client-centered] consultation is for the consultant to provide the consultee with the capability to deal with the client. The two primary aspects of the consultant-consultee relationship [in this form of consultation] are that the consultee will receive advice that can be offered immediately to the client and, through the process of consultation, will develop the capability to deal with similar problems in the future without a consultant's help. (Behavior Science Corporation, 1973, p. 30).

A secondary and derivative objective, in each instance of client-centered case consultation, is to increase the knowledge and skills of the consultee so that he can more effectively help the client. The problem lies in some lack of knowledge and/or skill on the part of the consultee.

In responding to a request for client-centered consultation, the consultant faces the same difficult problem faced by the supervisor. There is the problem of trying to understand the client's behavior and situation based primarily on descriptions supplied by the consultee. He is further often faced with the responsibility of suggesting a reasonable response to the client's situation based on data supplied by intermediaries. In resolving these difficulties the consultant may request to meet with the client directly. Actually, however, there appears to be limited use of such a procedure.

The following responses to the Kadushin-Buckman inquiry regarding the respondents' most recent consultation assignment are illustrative of the type of client-centered case consultations provided by social work consultants.

A consultant affiliated with a community mental health agency consulted with the principal of a junior high school about a student who was exposing himself.

The director of a medical social service unit consulted with a physician in a hospital emergency room around planning for an eight-month-old abused child.

A school social worker consulted with a paraprofessional in an inpatient mental health facility regarding diagnosis of and treatment planning for a runaway teen-age female.

A director of outpatient services in a public mental health facility consulted with a group of parents of twins in regard to parenting of twins.

A school social worker consulted with an elementary school teacher as to how she could best deal with the father of one of her students who is apparently mentally ill and who has been sending "suggestive" notes and gifts via the child.

A social work consultant with no agency affiliation consulted with a charge nurse in a nursing home about the sexual and aggressive behavior of one of her geriatric patients.

The chief psychiatric social worker in a community mental health center consulted with a social worker in a probation department with regard to the crisis situation of a homeless adolescent.

The social services consultant of a family service agency consulted with the designated social service worker in a skilled nursing facility concerning the management of a patient with severe paranoid ideation.

A chief social worker consulted with the head nurse of a free-standing hemodialysis center about the problems of helping their patients achieve better psychological and vocational rehabilitation.

A clinical Social Worker III consulted with a doctor in a pediatric clinic about the problem of developing workable treatment plans for an adolescent with dysfunctional family relationships.

A social services consultant in a public child welfare agency consulted with a lawyer regarding social agency procedures and requirements for adoption.

A supervisor of individual and group therapy in a voluntary child guidance clinic consulted with a teacher in a day care center about a child's inarticulate and isolated behavior.

The medical social work consultant in a public medical social work agency consulted with a social worker in a county welfare department regarding problems created by the parents' nonacceptance of treatment for a handicapped child.

2. *Consultee-centered case consultation.* The content of the consultation is, once again, a problem related to a client or a client group. However, in this type of consultation the "consultant focuses his main attention on trying to understand the nature of the consultee's difficulty with the case and in trying to help him remedy this" (Caplan, 1970, p. 32). The target of charge is the consultee. The consultee's difficulty with the client is utilized

as a lever for working toward change in the consultee. The objective here is primarily to modify the consultee's attitudes and behavior so that he can, secondarily, more effectively help the client. The problem lies in the way the consultee relates to his client, and consultee change is the primary, immediate intent of the procedure which has better client service as an ultimate consequence.

A worker has difficulty in understanding and accepting unmarried mothers; a worker has a problem in helping a black client because the worker's perception is distorted by a pervasive tendency to stereotype; a worker rejects an adolescent school dropout as a consequence of displacement of hostility deriving from his relationships to his own children; the worker is made anxious by a client who wants to discuss plans for an abortion.

The resistance, perceptual distortions, and affective displacements that adversely affect worker-client interaction and which stem from the worker's internalized conflicts are the subject matter for consultee-centered consultation. The consultant helps in the "dissolution of a derivative conflict [as manifested] primarily in the consultee's work ego functioning" (Hitchcock and Mooney 1969, p. 358).

In consultee-centered consultation the aim is to reduce the problems the consultee has in dealing with the client by using the discussion of the client's difficulties as a vehicle to enhance consultee self-awareness and self-understanding.

This source of difficulty, identified as a problem of "theme interference," is given considerable prominence in mental health consultation literature. It is defined as a "personal problem displaced onto the work situation producing temporary ineffectuality and loss of emotional stability in dealing with the work field" (Caplan 1970, p. 145). The "theme," whose interference the consultant seeks to resolve, is an "emotionally toned cognitive constellation" which results in the worker's perceptual distortion of the client in his situation. It is a "continuing representation" of a personal, unresolved problem faced by the consultee.

Consultee-centered consultation presupposes a rather sustained period of contact between consultant and consultee which permits the consultant to perceive the manifestation of "theme interference" in a sufficient variety of instances so as to confirm the inferences connecting job problems and personal problems. Some continuity of contact might also be regarded as a necessary prerequisite for effecting change in the consultee's attitudes and behavior. Consultee-centered consultation, as was noted in chapter 2, most directly raises the question of the distinction between consultation and therapy.

Here, as in supervision, there is the recognition that since the worker himself is the principal instrumentality in offering service it is necessary to be concerned with personal functioning as it directly affects professional functioning. The recognition that the consultant's concern with work-related consultee personal problems is both necessary and legitimate is conditioned by three provisos. First, the need to include these matters in consultation discussions is made explicit so that it is both understood and accepted by the consultee; secondly, the movement in consultation should logically be from client-centered consultation to consultee-centered consultation; and thirdly, any discussion of the attributes, characteristics, and problems of the consultee should be explicitly related to the work problem which is the concern of the consultation.

The following responses to the Kadushin-Buckman inquiry regarding the respondents' most recent consultation assignment are illustrative of the type of consultee-centered case consultation provided by social workers.

A psychiatric social worker consulted with the attending physician in a neonatal intensive care unit in helping him to handle his feelings about seriously ill infants.

A psychiatric social worker consulted with a lay counselor in a counseling service for women concerning her feelings of inadequacy and insecurity regarding responsibility for counseling.

A school social worker consulted with a junior high school teacher regarding his concerns over his punitive feelings toward disruptive students.

A consultant with no agency affiliation consulted with a doctor who was having a problem in informing his patients of their terminal illness.

The director of consultation and education of a voluntary mental health agency consulted with a rape action center volunteer about how to handle her task of being with a six-year-old during the questioning of the youngster by the authorities.

A public health social worker consultant in a state health department consulted with a medical social worker in a children's hospital regarding problems she was having in fitting into the action in the infants' intensive care unit program.

3. *Program-centered administrative consultation.* The content of the consultation "is in the area of planning and administration— how to develop a new program or to improve an existing one" (Caplan, 1970, p. 33). The target of change is the agency, its functions, programs, administration. The problem lies in the organization and/or administration of the agency. Instead of better understanding of the case situation and plans for case management which result in client-centered or consultee-centered case consultation, program-centered administrative consultation results in better understanding of the organization and plans for administrative action.

MacLennan, Quinn, and Shroeder (1975) have described mental health program-centered administrative consultation. They define it as dealing with problems concerned with the planning, development, management, and coordination of services directly or indirectly affecting the mental health of the community. . . . some examples of program consultation are: a city demonstration agency director requests consultation and technical assistance in planning the mental health components of a Model Cities program; the head of a city health department seeks advice in setting up a mental health program within his service; a hospital administrator requests help in establishing a psychiatric wing; a personnel director in a factory needs advice on dealing with a high rate of absenteeism; a civic group seeks assistance in organizing preschool nursery programs as an anti-poverty measure; or a legislator seeks aid in drafting a mental health service bill. These are among the kinds of program challenges a mental health consultant can expect to meet. (pp. 6, 7)

If client-centered consultation is concerned with changing client attitudes and behavior, and if consultee-centered consultation is concerned with changing the worker's attitudes and behavior, program-centered administrative consultation is concerned with effecting changes in the system in which client and worker carry out their transactions. A client-centered consultant might help the teacher-consultee plan a program of activities for a retarded child; a consultee-centered consultant might help the teacher-consultee deal with her negative, rejecting attitudes toward a retarded child; a program-centered consultation might help a school administrator-consultee consider open classroom procedures, or changes in the grading system which might make the school a more hospitable learning climate for retarded children.

Client-centered consultation requires a diagnostic understanding of the client; consultee-centered consultation requires a diagnostic understanding of the worker; program-centered consultation requires a diagnostic understanding of the organization and those processes, procedures, and structural defects which hamper optimal performance of organizational tasks.

Program-centered administrative consultation is directed

toward offering help in originating, planning, modifying, and implementing programs and program administration through the application of expertise in administrative processes and social systems dynamics.

Program-centered administrative consultation may grow out of the client-centered consultation experience. A number of client-centered conferences may present similar recurrent problems faced by clients. The cluster of problems may indicate to the consultant some deficiencies in the program to which he might then call the agency's attention.

Client-centered consultation comes closest to the traditional type of consultation encountered in medicine, psychiatry, and law. It is the type of consultation with which most consultees are likely to be familiar. It is closest to the casework model in social work which focuses on effecting change in the client in dealing with a problem of psychosocial dysfunctioning. Client-centered consultation is regarded as primarily concerned with repair and remediation of breakdown.

Program-centered consultation is closer to the social action systems change model in social work. The locus of the difficulties encountered by the client is presumed to be in the defects and inequities of the institutional arrangements of society and/or the failures in the service-delivery systems of help-offering agencies. Program-centered consultation is seen as having greater preventive potential than other types of consultation.

In line with an increasing emphasis on social action and prevention in the late 1960s and early 1970s there was increasing exhortation to move from an investment of time and energy on client-centered consultation to greater concern with program-centered consultation (Costin 1975).

The following responses to the Kadushin-Buckman inquiry regarding the respondents' most recent consultation assignment are illustrative of the type of program-centered administrative consultation provided by social workers.

A school social worker consulted with principals and counselors of the school district about developing guidelines for student records to meet the requirements of the Buckley Amendment.

The executive director of a voluntary social agency consulted with a citizens group interested in setting up a new agency to use paraprofessionals to counsel in life-threatening behavior.

The director of social services of a medical social work agency consulted with a hospital administrator in establishing a department of social service in his hospital.

A supervisor in a public child welfare agency consulted with the deputy administrator of a juvenile institution as to the best use of staff time in offering services to seventy-five youngsters during a four- or five-week detention stay.

The supervisor of the Division of Child Care, Institution and Group Homes and Child Placing Agencies in a public child welfare agency consulted with the administrator of a child care institution about the minimum standards for state licensure to operate the facility.

A social work consultant with no agency affiliation consulted with the director of a social agency with forty-three branches who wanted to know how to identify, recruit, train, and use volunteer leadership for board and nonboard committees.

A public health social work consultant offered consultation to a hospital social service director on setting up controls for peer auditing and assessing productivity of staff.

A social worker who held the position of assistant director of the Institute of Government in a public university consulted with the city manager and city attorney in a municipality of some 50,000 population about redesigning the local Human Relations Commission.

A psychiatric social worker affiliated with a mental health center consulted with a group of social workers and psychologists in a child guidance clinic on the problem of modifying a brief psychotherapy program.

The social work coordinator of a voluntary mental health agency consulted with a chamber of commerce executive concerning a plan to establish a child care program for employees.

The chief of social services of a public mental health unit consulted with the director of a state school for the mentally retarded to interpret standards for qualification as an intermediate care facility to qualify for federal funds.

A faculty member of a university school of social work consulted with the executive director of a public children's institution to help alleviate seriously constrictive child care practices which had received negative attention in the press and state legislature.

A medical social worker consulted with the charge nurse in a nursing home with regard to meeting the requirements of including a social work consultant on the agency staff.

An associate professor at a school of social work consulted with the executive director of a family service travelers aid agency concerning expansion of an outreach program to be funded through United Way.

A school social worker consulted with administrators in a high school about formulating a program to meet the needs of teen-age mothers who were students at the school.

A social work consultant in a public state health department consulted with the administrative staff of a Medicare certified home-health agency as to procedures necessary to insure conformity with Medicare regulations.

A social work program review specialist consulted with the unit director of a methadone maintenance program regarding the process of keeping patient records in a manner that would prove optimally useful to staff.

The group home coordinator of a private child welfare agency consulted with an administrator of an agency seeking to establish a group home program for adolescents.

A senior consultant on government relations in a community organization, planning, and development agency consulted with United Way administration regarding purchase of service contracts for social services under Title XX.

A special assistant in a public mental health agency met with administrators and direct-services staff of a mental health center in helping to develop a program of services and mental health education in rural communities.

A social work consultant with no agency affiliation consulted with the administrator of a scientific laboratory regarding establishing a counseling program for employees.

4. *Consultee-centered administrative consultation.* Once again the content of consultation is in the area of agency program and administration. But, here, as in consultee-centered consultation, the consultees themselves are the target of change. The consultant, using his knowledge of agency administration social systems, complex organizations and bureaucratic phenomena, formal and informal organizational structure, the patterns of organizational communication and decision-making, elucidates and attempts to remedy those factors operating in consultee interaction and interpersonal relationships which "interfere with their grappling with their tasks" (Caplan 1970, p. 33) of agency development, agency service, and program change. The problem lies in the interpersonal relationships of people who make up the agency, and consultation results in planning changes in the human relations aspects of the organization. As a result of consultation, agency morale might be improved, turnover reduced, communication between staff made freer and more open, the extent of intra-organizational participatory democracy in-

creased, the atmosphere of interpersonal relations in the organization more humanized.

If the targets of program-centered consultation are the organizational apparatus and structural arrangements, the targets of consultee-centered administrative consultation are the human beings who make up the organization.

The following responses to the Kadushin-Buckman inquiry regarding the respondents' most recent consultation assignment are illustrative of the type of consultee-centered administrative consultations provided by social workers.

A psychiatric social worker in a public mental health unit consulted with homemakers in the local department of social services in helping them clarify their responsibilities vis-à-vis the mentally ill in the home.

A child welfare supervisor consulted with social workers and psychologists at a residential treatment center in helping them accept group treatment approaches to children, parents, and cottage staff.

A staff development consultant in a public welfare agency consulted with groups of social workers in county welfare departments about the problems of managing their jobs in relation to Title XX.

A social work institutional consultant met with the director of child care of a private group home for children concerning the problems presented by the pending resignation of a set of cottage parents.

The service representative in a public assistance agency consulted with social work supervisors regarding staff morale problems associated with budget cuts and anticipated staff reductions.

A social work consultant consulted with a group of mental health secretaries on interoffice problems and training needs.

The personnel officer and staff development consultant in a public agency consulted with a group of agency supervisors on the problem of work-load disruption by employees failing to follow agency regulations.

The family life educator in a family service agency consulted with a police chief in a small township about education and treatment resources to alleviate marital problems of members of the police force.

A medical social work consultant consulted with an agency administrator in regard to problems of staff morale and lowered productivity.

5. *Advocacy consultation.* It has been suggested that Caplan's classification fails to include another distinct type of consultation identified as advocacy consultation. Advocacy consultation involves a strong commitment to making change in the system for which consultation is being offered.

Unlike the more neutrally oriented typical consultant, the advocacy consultant has a value-centric, partisan approach and is conscious of the value he deliberately wants to propagate, of the changes he thinks are desirable. The advocacy consultant's loyalty is not to the system which hires him but to his ideology and to those groups in the system whose needs are favored by his ideology.

The objectives of the advocacy consultant generally involve a redistribution of power and rewards in the system he seeks to reform. The process employed in achieving these objectives is, once again, different from those generally employed in consultation. It may involve the deliberate intensification of tension and conflict and direct-action approaches, including creative disruption.

The advocacy consultant may claim that there is no neutrality in consultantship, that consultancy aligned and cooperating with agency administration is a partisan activity in support of an established order, or of the elements of that order that control a particular organization (Chesler and Arnstein 1970, p. 23).

Since administrators usually have the prerogative of making the ultimate decision regarding inviting a consultant into the system, since the administrators have to make available the resources—personnel, time, money, office space—which would make possible the work of the consultant, it is not very likely that a consultant whose views were decidedly and explicitly at variance with that of the administration would gain access to the system. The likelihood of remaining in the system is also related to continuing lack of serious conflict between consultant and agency administration. To be effective, such a consultant would need to find allies within the system, staff groups oriented toward the charge being advocated, and/or with community groups involved in the system's operation and who have leverage for effecting change. The advocacy consultant may have to initiate consultation and may have to operate without full organizational sanction. These would appear to be some of the problems faced by advocacy consultation. These serious constraints may help explain the fact that no responses to the Kadushin-Buckman inquiry were received which illustrate social work advocacy consultation.

Types of Consultation: Frequency of Concern

There is a question with regard to the frequency with which the various types of consultation are engaged in by social work and mental health consultants. There is a heavy emphasis in the mental health consultation literature on consultee-centered consultation. However, the available research tends to suggest that only a limited amount of consultation effort is awarded to this type of consultation. The type of consultation most frequently offered, by far, appears to be client-centered consultation.

While the definitions of categories are slightly different from those used by Caplan, a national tabulation of types of consultation offered by community mental health center staff shows case consultation as unequivocally the most frequent kind of consultation offered. Forty-seven percent of the total consultation-education staff time went to case consultation (Bass 1974, p. 2). Since case consultation is defined as "consultation regarding an identifiable individual, client or family unit for the primary purpose of diagnosis, treatment and/or disposition," it is clearly the equivalent of Caplan's "client-centered consultation."

By contrast, "a total of 22 percent of staff time was devoted to a combination of staff development or continued education." The "staff development" component of this category, which includes only a part of the total 22 percent of staff time devoted voted to this category, is defined as consultation "for the primary purpose of skill building or personal growth of the consultee." It is the equivalent of Caplan's "consultee-centered consultation."

In the national study of community mental health center consultation to twenty school districts it was found that client- or case-centered consultation was, "by far," the most frequent kind of consultation offered, being provided by 57 percent of the consultants (Behavior Science Corporation, 1973, p. 117).

A study which solicited 233 critical incidents in consultation from 24 guidance counselor consultants and 103 teacher consultees showed that only 8 percent of the consultations reported were consultee-centered consultations concerned with helping the teacher understand herself. Some 71 percent were focused on client problems. Furthermore, the consultation concerned with helping the teacher understand herself (consultee-centered consultation) was more likely to be regarded as ineffective compared with consultations designed to help the teachers understand the behavior of their students (client-centered consultation) (Splete 1968, p. 131). Splete's findings are supported by Iscoe *et al.* (1967), Mazade (1974), Millar (1966), and Woody (1974), all of whom found, in researching the consultants' activities, that mental health consultants were more heavily focused on client-centered consultation as compared with either consultee-centered consultation or program-centered consultation. Nagler and Cook (1973) collected data on 251 consultation visits by 11 mental health consultants to schools in 8 different towns. "The consultations were highly case focused (75 percent) with about two-thirds of the problems raised by the consultee pertaining to the individual student problems in school, in contrast to only 12 percent pertaining to programmatic issues'" (p. 246). Only one percent of the consultations were with school superintendents, and in 84 percent of the consultations the consultant provided the service requested by the consultee. There was, for the most part, limited concern with institutional or system change on the part of the consultants.

The orientation of the consultants, which tended to protect and maintain the system while attempting to change the child, was, however, not surprising. The consultants, all staff members of a mental health clinic, "functioned primarily as clinicians when not in the field. . . . The staff must have felt more comfortable functioning in the quasi-clinician role—as a case consultant—than in the non-clinical role, as an agent of social change" (p. 250).

The consultant's preferences were sustained and reinforced by the consultee's expectations and perceptions. Identifying the consultants as representatives of the mental health clinic the teachers perceived them as clinicians and expected them to operate in this role.

The greater frequency of client-centered consultation may result from the fact that this type of consultation is more comfortable for the consultee than is consultee-centered consultation. In the former the consultee is concerned with someone else's problems, failings, inadequacies; in the latter, the consultee has to share his own problems, failings, inadequacies.

The reports available of systems change efforts on the part of consultants are far less dramatic than is suggested by the exhortations to reform radically a pathogenic, inequitable social environment. Anderson (1976) describes in detail a consultation program which had both a case consultation remedial-reparative approach for school children in difficulty and a program-centered consultation with a preventive systems-change approach to the school systems. The consultants systems-change approach efforts, however, turn out to be a rather elaborate in-service training program to change teacher attitudes and approach to students. Anderson notes that the general emphasis on remedial-reparative case consultation is only partly the consequence of the consultant's ideological preferences. It is also because "school systems are often unwilling to involve themselves in anything other than case consultation" (p. 85).

There is more limited data available on the types of consultation requested by, and of, social workers as consultees and consultants. In a study by Aiken (1957) of psychiatric consultation to family service agencies it is clear that case-centered consultation was most frequently requested. Help was asked regarding client diagnosis and psychodynamics, client treatment and management.

Detailed questionnaires submitted by thirty-nine social work consultants to nursing homes resulted in the finding that case consultation was the most frequent type of consultation offered by the consultants (Austin and Fosberg, 1976). Most of the consultant's time was spent with nursing home staff and residents. "Little time was spent with nursing home administrators or community representatives" (p. 13).

On the other hand, a study by Tetreault (1968) of the objectives of school social work consultants indicated their tendency to see consultation in consultee-centered consultation terms. The concern of these consultants was on meeting the consultee's affective needs for support and abreaction.

In an effort to determine more definitively the frequency with which the different types of consultation were engaged in by social work consultants, the Kadushin-Buckman questionnaire asked the respondents to categorize the consultation situations which they encountered in terms of the four types of consultation as described by Caplan. A paraphrase of the distinctive focus of each type, along with the frequency with which each type is encountered by the 483 consultants participating in the study, is given in Table 3.

It is clear that these social work consultants, like consultants in related disciplines, most frequently encountered problems of client-centered consultation and problems of consultee-centered

Table 3 Frequency with Which Particular Types of Consultation Requests are Encountered, in Percent

$(N = 483)$

Types of Consultation	Frequency		
	Frequently	Occasionally	Rarely or Never
1. Client-centered consultation: helping the consultee deal with work problems he has encountered with clients about diagnosis, treatment, case disposition, etc.	36.4	19.4	16.3
2. Consultee-centered consultation: helping the consultee with his own hang-ups, inter- and intrapersonal difficulties which make for problems in working with clients	11.0	32.0	34.0
3. Program-centered administrative consultation: helping the consultee's agency make administrative policy changes to increase its effectiveness, developing, planning, implementing, and researching agency policy and programs	33.0	23.0	20.0
4. Consultee-centered administrative consultation: helping to change the nature of staff interpersonal relationships, cliques, communication barriers, etc., so that the consultee's agency can operate more effectively	20.0	26.0	30.0
Total	100.0	100.0	100.0

consultation least frequently. This is, as has been noted, contrary to the heavy emphasis given to problems of consultee-centered consultation in the literature.

Table 3 further notes that there is considerable concern with program-centered and administrative consultation on the part of the social work consultants. As a consequence of such requests the respondents in the study indicated that their consultees were often likely to be agency administrators or supervisors as well as with workers in direct-service positions, such as caseworkers, nurses, teachers, and so on.

The Content of Social Work Consultation

The social work literature provides some details on the contribution that social workers make in offering consultation. Reporting on the work of such consultants in the public health and medical services, Insley (1959) says:

> The social work consultant focuses on helping the consultee to understand and deal more effectively with psychosocial factors related to health and disease in individual case situations. . . . This may involve giving of information about social services and social agencies, assistance in selecting appropriate social services, exploration of methods of reference, and help in understanding how to cooperate with social workers in other community agencies. (p. 217)

Alt's (1959) report on the use of medical social workers in a prepaid health insurance plan in New York City also suggests that sharing experts' knowledge regarding social service resources was a principal contribution of such consultants.

Social workers acted as consultants to nurses in a project concerned with evaluating the treatment of schizophrenics in a home setting:

Since only one of the five nurses had previous psychiatric nursing experience, the nurses needed support and guidance in working with their patients. The responsibility of helping seriously ill patients in the home setting, who otherwise would most certainly have been hospitalized, resulted in serious emotional strain for the nurses. Their major fears centered about whether or not they had said or done the "right thing" in regard to a problem that had been presented by a patient or family. In this respect the social worker had to introduce the nurses to some basic casework techniques in dealing with the patient and family. Also, the nurses needed someone who could take direct action in the event that a patient or family presented a problem necessitating immediate referral to a social agency. (Albini, 1968, p. 116)

Warriner (1949), in a rather exceptional reference to consultation to administration regarding personality-related staff problems, notes that the division of a state board of health

made free use of the psychiatric social worker's (consultant's) technical knowledge in order to gain insight into the personality structure of staff members whose personal adjustments affect their professional performance. Efforts have been made to modify the working situation so that the individual supervisors and staff nurses have asked the consultant for help in understanding each other so that they might work together better. (p. 397)

In discussing social work consultation with school personnel, Moss (1976) details the contribution which social workers supposedly can make:

Because of his knowledge of the dynamics of personality and the interactional process, the social work consultant is in an excellent position to help the educational staff achieve a better understanding of the psychological dimensions of the learning process. By understanding the emotional meaning of the educator's concerns, the social work consultant can sensitively and purposefully intervene

help clarify any confusion the teacher may experience relating to
his role and can broaden his perspective on troublesome issues.

The clarification of the existing pressures, their sources and
their psychological impact, enables educators to develop a heightened awareness of their own emotional responses along with an
increased understanding of the multiple pressures on children and
parents. (p. 146)

It has been noted that social work consultants often carry
licensing and administrative review responsibilities in addition
to those activities which reflect the more traditional connotations
of consultation. The Civil Service announcement of one large
state for the position Social Service Consultant II indicates this
in outlining the duties of the position as follows:

> *As a program development specialist:* participates in the develop-
> ment of new policies, procedures, and methods for such welfare
> programs as Aid to Needy Children, Old Age Security, Medical
> Care, Child Welfare Services, Adoptions, Aged and Children's Insti-
> tution Licensing, Aid to Totally Disabled, Aid to Needy Blind, and
> Prevention of Blindness. *As an area representative:* analyzes and
> evaluates the quality, quantity, and effectiveness of operations and
> social services in the local administration of public welfare and their
> conformance to policies, standards, long-range objectives, and sound
> professional principles; identifies needed changes and makes appro-
> priate recommendations in view of local needs, economic factors,
> and local attitudes. *As a licensing representative:* licenses 24-hour
> care institutions for children and the aged and day care facilities for
> children; evaluates, in relation to State standards, the programs of
> such facilities to determine the extent to which they meet the psy-
> chological, social, and emotional needs of children and aged persons;
> and does other work as required.

The particular expertise contributed by the social work consultant may be along methodological lines (specialist in social
work research), in specialized settings (specialist in residential

treatment centers), in some particular problem area (specialist in teen-age unmarried motherhood), or in some special therapeutic procedure (behavioral modification).

The expertise may be very narrowly focused, combining a variety of different kinds of specializations; that is, the consultant may be a specialist in social work research regarding behavior modification procedures applied to unmarried teen-age mothers living in a residential treatment center.

Responses obtained by the Kadushin-Buckman survey indicate that some of the consultants are consultants by virtue of specialized knowledge learned on the job in highly specialized positions. It is this expertise rather than that developed by professional training in social work that is used as the basis for consultation.

Job titles of social workers who have consultation responsibilities indicate specialized expertise. Thus social work consultants hold titles such as program specialist, developmental disabilities specialist, adoptions specialist, family foster care specialist, welfare services specialist, Medicaid procedures specialist, senior psychotherapist and consultant on problems of the elderly, principal child welfare specialist, program evaluation specialist, licensing specialist.

Summary

Situations in which social workers acted as consultees were presented, as was the professional designation of the consultants to social workers. This was followed by a discussion of those situations in which social workers were called on to act as consultants. The contribution of the social work consultants to their consultees and the nature of the structural arrangements for social work consultation were reviewed. Four types of consultation were outlined—client-centered, consultee-centered, program-centered, and consultee-program-centered consultation. The research regarding the frequency with which the various types of consultation were offered was summarized.

Chapter Four

The Consultation Process:
Contact, Entry, Contract

Consultation, like supervision, is a process. It involves a series of sequential steps designed to achieve the objective of the contact and, like all processes, it has a beginning, a middle, and an end. Each phase of the process has some distinctive characteristics and each phase requires the performance of certain clearly defined tasks by either the consultant or the consultee and in some instances both.

Process varies somewhat with the type of consultation offered. For purposes of simplicity we have selected client-centered case consultation as the prototype for our discussion of process. The selection is justified on the basis of the fact that this is probably the most frequent type of consultation requested and offered in social work.

Contact

Consultants and consultee organizations make contact in a variety of ways. The organization, or agency, having identified a need for consultation then seeks a consultant whose specialized expertise relates to the identified need. This may involve judicious inquiry among people who are reputed to know something about the consultants who might be available. Sometimes an appeal is made to the staff of national organizations who might be familiar with the work of possible consultants.

The Child Welfare League of America statement of standards for the different child welfare services explicitly notes the qualification of consultants which might be used as criteria for selection. They indicate that "specialists retained by the agency should meet requirements for membership in the standard-setting organization in their own field," a validation of the consultant's expertise. They should be willing and able to "identify with the goals and philosophy of the agency"; provide service in such a manner that they form an integral part of the total service of the agency; be willing to "collaborate with the other professional workers and have [their] specific service coordinated through the social work or [agency] director" (Child Welfare League of America, 1975, p. 88).

The consultant may operate as an individual entrepreneur whose technical assistance is hired and paid for by the consultee agency. Faculty members of schools of social work, or highly visible practitioners, are invited to consult on this basis. Some member of the consultee agency has heard the social worker speak at some meeting, or has read his published material, or has served on some national committee with the prospective consultant. He has identified the consultant as very knowledgeable about some aspect of social work—mental retardation, institutional care, geriatrics, research, transracial adoptions, behavioral modification, and so forth. The agency encountering a problem regarding this particular aspect of its work responds to the recommendation of the staff member who is acquainted with the work of the consultant and invites him for consultation. In most such instances consultation is a secondary rather than a primary activity of the consultant. The consultant operates most frequently as an individual, although on occasion he may be a member of a consultant team.

The consultant may operate as a staff member of an organization such as a mental health center or a state agency which provides a consultation service and often pays the salary of the consultant. In some instances consultation is the primary activity of the professional, and she holds the title of consultant.

Sometimes the consultee agency is already in contact with the consultant but in her performance of a different function. Thus the licensing agent or the representative of a national standard-setting organization may be in contact with the agency for the purpose of licensing or review of standards. The consultant may already be in contact with the agency in the role of state or federal administrative review functionary. The agency may voluntarily request a change in relationship to consultant-consultee.

Fifty-five percent of the respondents to the Kadushin-Buckman (1971) Survey indicated that the principal avenue for contact between themselves and the consultee was through the agencies with which the consultants were affiliated. Consultees made contact with the agency in requesting consultation, and as employees of the agency, the consultants were assigned responsibility for meeting the request. In 18 percent of the cases the prospective consultee made contact directly with the consultant, having identified him/her through other consultees with wom the consultant had previously worked. Thirteen percent of the respondents indicated that the consultee was generally referred by other professionals. Less frequently consultants become known through their writings or as a result of seminar or lecture presentations.

Contact for consultation is not always entirely voluntary.

For instance, in identifying the conditions under which consultation is initiated, 30.3 percent of the respondents to the Kadushin-Buckman survey indicated that frequently "my consultees are under some administrative constraints to seek my consultation" and an additional 33.4 percent indicated that this condition obtained "occasionally." This is related to the fact that some 38 percent of the consultants were paid staff members of an agency which had administrative, regulatory, or licensing responsibilities to the professionals or agencies to which consultation was given. Consultation, then, for a third of the respondents was a component of the administrative supervisory functions of one agency vis-à-vis another, and the consultees might have felt some administrative constraints to seek and accept such consultation.

All of these contact contingencies have in common the fact that they are initiated by the consultee. Contact may, however, be initiated by the consultants or by the consulting organization soliciting a consultee. It is, in effect, an outreach effort on the part of the consultant in an attempt to interest a prospective consultee in using consultation.

The situation is typical of those agencies, like the mental health centers, which are mandated to offer a consultative service. They are then placed in a "position of seeking out community programs which would be willing to permit the consultant to use them as objects of consultation. . . . These consultees [are] in a particularly advantageous position of a knowledgeable buyer being pressured to accept a full set of services" (McClung and Stunden, 1972, p. 38). As in the analogous case of the involuntary client of a social agency, the consultees, at the beginning of the process, may not have any explicit awareness of the need for consultation. In the case of consultation offered by community health centers, the question of whose needs are being served is made more ambiguous by the fact that the cost of the service is generally assumed by the consultant rather than the consultees.

Reports confirm the fact that entry for consultation is a problem in those instances where the consultee has not articulated a need for consultation and where the consultant initiates the contact. One mental health center program using social workers and psychologists as consultants found that in offering consultation without invitation they had to contact sixteen schools to gain entrance to thirteen, only eleven of which ultimately used the service (Horn *et al.*, 1969).

The ticket for admission to the consultee agency is often the need to provide direct service to the prospective consultee organization before consultation is accepted. The consultants can establish their utility value to the consultees in this way and counter some initial skepticism and resistance.

Rabiner *et al.* (1970) report the total initial failure of an offer to local agencies of client-centered consultation by a hospital department of psychiatry. It was only after a direct-service program was offered as the prime service to the community that some requests for consultation were received. It was concluded that

> Psychiatric consultation will be accepted and utilized in a community only to the extent that basic direct services are already in effect and that the services can be delivered in an atmosphere of trust. In highly disadvantaged communities, particularly black ghetto areas where crucial direct services are woefully lacking and where the level of fear and suspicion is high, it is essential that direct services be offered to meet the most immediate practical needs . . . before more indirect services such as consultation can be meaningfully introduced. (p. 1325)

Mannino (1964) reports a similar experience in the efforts of a mental health center to replace referral for direct service by consultation. The agencies resisted retaining primary responsibility of the care situation with the help of consultative services. The community was able to move to a somewhat greater readiness to use consultative services only after the mental health center indicated a greater willingness to accept the request for direct service.

The entry as a direct-service practitioner can be employed as a lever in establishing a consultative relationship. A psychologist offering direct services to a school system accepted the request for diagnosis and treatment

> but then carefully involved the consultee in the interaction between himself and the client. In method, what he did was to train the referring teacher in the role of consultee, to report back to him as consultant, and wherever possible to be actively involved in management and treatment. After a while he was able to establish the policy that he would accept referrals only from school personnel who would be responsible for follow-up with the client, and again, with time, he was able to shift emphasis to the consultees. (Cohen, 1963, p. 75)

In another instance entry for consultation resulted from an offer of direct service and informal familiarization:

> In one elementary school, although the pupil services staff reported considerable stress because of the relationship between the school principal and his faculty and below-average performance of the children, the principal decided that he did not wish a regular relationship with the mental health consultant. He did allow the consultant to attend building conferences once a month and provided space for him to treat any children who were referred. The consultant came to the school 4 hours a week to undertake evaluation and therapy with children and their parents individually or in groups.
>
> The consultant, however, was not satisfied with this arrangement. . . . The consultant set out to gain the confidence of the principal. Each time he came to the school he visited the principal's office and spent a few minutes with him informally. He began to lunch at the school getting to know the teachers in a casual way as well as on a more formal basis. After about a month he asked the

principal to lunch with him at which time he discussed his progress.
This became a regular monthly arrangement and after five or six
such meetings the principal began to discuss some of his problems
with the consultant. They were now on a friendly basis and the
meetings increased to twice a month. This frequency was sustained
over the next year and resulted in the principal using the consultant
to help him work out his conflicts with some of his staff, to develop
special programs for emotionally disturbed children and to study the
effect on the children of making the transition from a rural family
into a modern school environment. (MacLennan, 1975, p. 149)

Examples of unsolicited entry and the problems encountered by such consultation outreach efforts are discussed in
greater detail by Grossman and Quinlan (1972) and Pargament
(1977).

Success in reaching the initially "involuntary" consultee
seems to be predicated on a perception of consultation services
as adjunctive rather than as a substitute for the availability of adequate direct services. The willingness, however, to move in
this direction on the part of the agency offering consultation
must be predicated on some assessment to determine whether
direct service is being requested for a situation for which consultation might, in fact, be the more appropriate service.

Consultation may result from deliberate outreach efforts.

When a new [mental health] center was beginning to develop its
program, the director and senior staff visited the superintendent of
the local school district and his senior administrators. The director
stated that as the center was now responsible for the sound mental
health development of the children in the catchment area and as the
superintendent and his staff were responsible for the education of all
the children, it seemed appropriate to explore how the two agencies
could be most useful to each other. As one result of his visit, one
sub-area team met with the 12 local elementary school principals,
who asked the mental health staff to provide them with a seminar on
"disruptive children." This led the principals to invite the consul-

tants into their schools to teach them how to consult with their faculty on the management of mental health problems in the classroom. (MacLennan, 1974, p. 108)

Sometimes entry is the result of a series of successful approximations to consultation. Thus in

one instance a principal asked the consultant to do a different kind of task each time, i.e. interview a child or a parent, visit a classroom, make a referral, give a speech to the PTA, etc., until he finally became convinced that the consultant was concerned with helping and understanding the administrator and was not another prima donna from the superintendent's office concerned only with his special little project and his own professionally narcissistic satisfactions. (Berlin, 1974, p. 21)

The point of entry to a system which might advantageously use consultation but which has, as yet, expressed no felt need for the service can sometimes be through a more familiar, more acceptable service. Consultants may obtain entry to the staff as educators before being accepted as consultants. A series of lectures or leadership of staff discussion seminars may result in contact for consultation.

In one instance entry to the school system was expedited by demonstrating the utility value of consultation to the principal through an assertiveness training program for such administrators offered by the consultants (Smith, 1975).

Sometimes neither the consultee nor the consulting agency has identified the need for consultation, but the need is perceived by the community. "In one instance a PTA stimulated the administration to obtain consultation services and then paid out of their own funds to bring in a psychiatrist to meet with the teachers one afternoon every two weeks" (Berkowitz, 1975, p. 35).

Contact and entry may be administratively required. For a

time nursing homes were required to have social work consultation as a condition for Medicare reimbursement.

Daggett *et al.* (1974) describe the procedure used in gaining
entry to nursing homes for the aged by a team of consultants
composed of social workers and nurses. The consultation program initiated by a community mental health center was

> designed to offer additional knowledge about the psychological and
> social needs of the elderly, assist in program development to in-
> crease the elderly's social participation, encourage increased use of
> mental health resources in the community, assist the staff of the care
> facilities in dealing with their communications problems, and in-
> crease understanding of psychiatric terminology and treatment. (p.
> 171)

The procedure in initiating contact involved describing

> the service at a conference of the Metropolitan Area Nursing Home
> Association and in a letter to the nursing homes; we received a wide
> response. Nursing homes that did not respond were contacted by
> telephone. As the project progressed, we developed and distributed
> to care facilities a brief folder outlining the project's objectives and
> procedures. At the end of the year a direct invitation to participate
> had been extended to all homes in the catchment area. (p. 171)

A more detailed study of the impact on schools of programs
of consultation provided by twenty different community mental
health centers throughout the country found that the most successful approach observed was based on the center's

> contacting senior administrative staff of a school district to indicate
> the availability of mental health consultation services and requesting
> a series of meetings to explain the full range of services which could
> be provided and their implications for the school district. Through
> these joint meetings, there is an opportunity for school personnel to
> understand better what it is they could receive, determine its ul-

timate utility in the educational process for their children, decide whether or not such services could, in fact, contribute to the broad educational goals of the school district, and to determine the approximate level of effort or size of program which would be best for the district. Through these meetings, the school district becomes more comfortable in dealing with mental health professionals and considerably more likely to allow the program of services to be initiated. The most successful programs observed also attempt to sign a contract with the school district, even if all the services are provided without charge. The purpose of the contract is to make a mutual commitment on both sides not only of approximate level of effort, but of the fact that the program is to be considered an integral part of the ongoing educational process. (Plog, 1974, pp. 58–59)

This detailed statement of approach illustrates some of the desirable principles of consultation contact which were recommended as a consequence of this nationwide study.

More effective consultation experiences are associated with deliberate coordinated planned entry to the consultee's domain rather than *ad hoc* consultations which evolve, piecemeal, into an equivocal program. There is active participation of the consultee agency administrators and staff in the development of the consultation program; there is subsequent communication and feedback not only to the consultees directly involved in ongoing consultation activities, but also to the administrative staff only indirectly involved. There are shared goals and expectations between consultants and consultees; there is a willingness to provide direct service as well as consultation on the part of the consultants. Credibility is established in the beginning by providing consultation in areas in which the consultant has confidence that some measure of success can be achieved.

Choice of Consultant

In deciding on the use of consultation one of the questions frequently debated by organizations is the advantage and disadvantage of using in-house consultants as against out-house consultants, the latter term being used advisedly and meaning a consultant from outside the organization.

As a "stranger" to the organization the outside consultant brings some special advantages. He comes with a broader, less parochial perspective on the problem. Agency personnel tend to take agency program assumptions and agency administrative arrangements for granted. They think within the organizational framework, its regulations, procedures, and traditions without being aware of these constraints. The consultant is not constricted, in his thinking, by these difficulties. As an outsider the consultant may more easily identify the crippling myths, the unproductive assumptions which guide the organization's operations and provide the basis for its "institutional neurosis." As Lippitt and Lippitt (1975) indicate, "The internal consultant is part of the client system and therefore may well be part of the problem" (p. 40).

The consultant comes without any political loyalties to any point of view or to any group in the agency. He has less vested interest in agency procedures since he will not be affected by any changes in agency procedures which are discernible. The fact that he is a stranger places him in a position of lesser risk. He can afford to say the "dirty word," to risk confrontation, because he will not, subsequently, have to live day to day with the perhaps nasty residual of such confrontation.

Since the consultant is here today and gone tomorrow the consultee may feel freed from some inhibition in sharing his less acceptable thinking and feelings with the consultant.

The outside consultant by virtue of his consultative status alone, aside from any expertise, thus has some valuable attributes which might be usefully exploited by the consultee agency in problem-solving. On the other hand, the outside consultant has to gain not only entry but acceptance in the organization. He works under the burden of not intimately knowing the organization's structure, mores, procedures, language. He is not always available to deal with "hot" issues as they arise for consultation and may have to be assigned less significant "can-wait" problems.

The inside consultant, on the other hand, has the problem of achieving credibility as a consultant. Aphorisms about "familiarity breeding contempt" and "a prophet without honor in his own country" point to the central disadvantage of the in-house consultant.

Consultants who represent an outside organization rather than operating as individual entrepreneurs are constrained by the mission of their organization, by the image their organization has in the community, by the relationship of their organization to the consultee's organization. The consultee-consultant relationship in this instance is not solely a relationship of individuals but also a relationship between their respective agencies as well. The consultant has to be aware of the fact that representing an outside organization has some implications for determining the nature of the consultation interaction.

Motives for Consultation

The way contact is made depends to some extent on the motives which lie behind the use of consultation. These are often multiply determined. The principal primary motive for consultation is the need for help with a work-related problem. This is the most appropriate motive. However, consultation may be motivated by a variety of reasons, some latent and rarely clearly expressed. These "secondary" functions of consultation are in the nature of "hidden agendas." The reasons are unrelated to problem-solving, to the use of consultants for the help they might provide in dealing with work-related problems. The contribution that the consultant makes in performing these "secondary" functions often derives from the perception of him as an objective, impartial expert having no vested interest in agency operation and, consequently, no ax of his own to grind. Here his status as an outsider is important. Thus, in policy conflicts between administration and significant subgroups in the agency or between administration and the board, consultation is requested in the hope that results can be used to support the administration's position.

A consultant's report might be used to justify agency policy change to the community. A decision in favor of the policy change may have been made, and the consultation is an afterthought to increase chances of its acceptance. The consultant gives the policy change the stamp of approval of a knowledgeable, disinterested observer. The situation is somewhat like that of the judge who instructed the jury to "go in there give him a fair trial and come out with a verdict of guilty."

A consultant may be employed to share the emotional burden of making a difficult decision. Agency and administration know what they want to do; may know, in fact, what they may have to do. However, they want somebody else whose opinion they respect to tell them that it is a good, desirable thing to do. This puts the onus for the decision partially on the shoulders of the consultant.

Engaging in consultation delays making a decision. Rather than coming to grips with the problem the agency, or the worker, may request consultation. He then has a valid, sanctioned reason for tabling the problem for a time. Consultation shares with research this possibility for temporizing in the face of a discomforting situation.

Employing a consultant has sometimes been cited as one of a series of delaying tactics in avoiding a decision. The Rules for Decision Avoidance include the following: "If you can avoid a decision do so; if you can't avoid a decision delay it. When it is not necessary to make a decision, it is necessary not to make a decision. If you can get somebody else to avoid a decision, don't avoid it yourself. If you cannot get one person to avoid the decision appoint a committee." In avoiding a decision as a member of a committee, hire a consultant to make a study.

A consultant may be wanted not so much for her expertise but because she has a relationship with, or access to, some resource in which the consultee agency is interested—a funding agency, a resource group, a prestigious national organization. Through consultants the consultee organization develops a tie to such resources, a better knowledge of how to tap such resources (Macarov et al., 1967).

An administrator may seek consultation because he needs the opportunity to discuss his problems with a knowledgeable, neutral outsider. The administrator is often the loneliest person in the agency. His discussions with any staff member of some of the problems he faces may trigger rivalry and rumors and exacerbate competition between different cliques in the agency. The administrator is able to talk freely to the consultant, however, without worrying about how this will affect the complicated network of relationships in the agency.

As Spencer and Croley (1963) note, the administrator

cannot afford to discuss all the things that bother him with members of his staff because he may show partiality or because it may shatter the illusion of the self-confident administrator. Formal and informal communication are limited to a degree that places a heavy psychological burden on him. Within the system there is virtually no one to whom he may turn for a free discussion of the issues upon which final decisions depend—the consultant is one of the few professional people in whom the administrator can confide with some assurance of understanding. (p. 64)

Consultants provide a noncompetitive, professional relationship with administrators. Roberts (1968) says that, as a consultant, "I found it important to remind myself that administrators like and often have needs for support, reassurance and recognition. Ultimately one of the most valuable contributions I could make was to prevent or alleviate their feelings of despair and discouragement as they struggled with massive social problems and apathetic communities" (p. 241).

In the case of newly developed projects, employment of high-status consultants has the effect of legitimizing the agency in the eyes of the professional community. The motive for consultation, then, is to assure such acceptance and support.

Where the prestige of the consultant's profession is higher in the public image than that of the profession which the agency represents, consultation may be sought for its prestige value. The consultant "lends" some of his prestige to the agency by virtue of his association with it. This consideration, rather than any expectation of help in problem-solving, may motivate the agency to arrange for consultation.

A similar motive may be a component of the individual consultee's request for consultation. The prestige-conferring motives of consultation may be inferred from results of a study of the relationship between social workers, psychiatrists and psychologists. "The social worker feels accepted and respected by the psychiatrist when he shares many professional activities with them. It is the social worker with little power who meets most often with them" (Zander, Cohen, and Stotland, 1966, p. 240).

Individual workers and supervisors may also have their own idiosyncratic motives for consultation in addition to, or in substitution of, motives related to problem-solving. Workers may request consultation with difficult clients—potential suicides, suspected psychotics, predelinquents—to share the responsibility for a difficult decision or to abdicate responsibility for the case. Consultation may be a way for the worker to seek help with his own personal problems. It may be a response to an effort to please a supervisor who is interested in pleasing the consultant.

Respondents in the Kadushin-Buckman survey were asked to indicate the frequency with which they encountered the variety of possible motives for consultation. Table 4 lists the motives and the frequency with which the consultants perceived them as operative.

Clearly, the most frequently cited (32 percent) motive for consultation, as perceived by the consultant, is that a problem encountered by the consultee requires the help of the consultant. The second most frequently (21 percent) cited motive is the desire on the part of the consultee to obtain an outsider's objective assessment of a problematic situation.

It might be noted that some noninstrumental motives for consultation receive a fair degree of mention as either "frequently" or "occasionally" operating. Thus consultation serves the purpose of sharing a difficult decision with the consultant, and consultation serves to alleviate the professional isolation of the consultee.

In distinguishing consultation from supervision, the point is often made that while supervision is an administrative requirement, consultation is entirely voluntary. However, it might be noted that consultants perceived the motive for consultation, operating "frequently" in 11 percent of the cases, as being in response to the administrative requirements of a certifying or accrediting agency with which the consultee has some relationship. In these instances one might question whether consultation was a voluntary choice.

While some of these motives may be termed "secondary" functions of consultation they are not any less important than the "primary" functions—and may, on occasion, be more important. Nor is it demeaning to the consultant to be used in this way. It is demeaning to the consultant only if he permits himself to be manipulated. Whatever conclusions the consultee may want from him, the consultant must be true to the best conclusions he can formulate. To follow Josh Billings's advice about advice— "Whenever I am asked for advice I try to find out what kind of advice is wanted and then I give it to them"—is ultimately fatal

Table 4 Frequency of Motives for Consultation As Perceived by the Consultant, in Percent

(N = 472)

Perceived Motive for Consultation	Frequency		
	Frequently	Occasionally	Rarely or Never
A problem is encountered with which the consultee needs the help of a consultant.	32.0	5.0	0.05
Consultation is motivated by a desire to obtain an outsider's objective assessment of a problematic situation.	21.0	11.4	4.0
Consultation serves the purpose of sharing responsibility for a difficult decision by the consultee with the consultant.	11.0	16.5	7.0
Consultation serves the purpose of alleviating professional isolation of consultee.	11.0	13.7	8.5
The use of consultation is motivated by compliance with the implicit or explicit requirements of a certifying or accrediting agency.	11.0	9.0	12.5
The consultee is interested in obtaining the consultant's support and approval for a decision, a course of action, already decided upon.	5.0	16.6	11.3
In seeking a grant or approval, accreditation, licensing of a program, the consultant's name and prestige are employed to increase the likelihood of a favorable decision.	4.0	9.0	17.5
The consultee is seeking an ally in the consultant in an intra-agency or interagency dispute.	3.0	13.0	16.0
Consultation provides a procedure for delaying action on a question of importance regarding agency policy.	1.0	5.5	2.3
Total	100.0	100.0	79.15

to the consultant. The very attribute which makes him a valuable political ally is compromised as a consequence. Only if those concerned with the consultation agree that he is an objective, impartial, uninterested "witness" can they accept his conclusions as that of a "nonadvocate."

The fact that the request for consultation is often multiply determined means that it is incumbent on the consultant to keep asking himself what is wanted from him and why. It requires that he be sensitive to the nature of agency politics so that he can be aware of how he might be being used.

A question which needs to be answered at this point in the process, after contact but before entry, is whether consultation is the procedure of choice for dealing with the prevailing situation. Careful consideration of this question may lead to the decision that the most desirable alternative is a formal program of in-service training, or more adequate supervision, or upgrading the requirements for entry-level positions rather than providing consultation resources to the staff. Consultation is inefficiently employed if it is used as a substitute for supervision or an inadequate in-service training program. It may be that what is needed is an increase in staff rather than in the ability of the current work force to handle more adequately the current caseload through consultation.

If it is decided that consultation is the alternative of choice, the individual consultant has to ask herself further whether she is the consultant of choice for this assignment. It may be that the nature of the consultant's orientation as to desirable procedures, goals, and objectives is philosophically at decided variance with the prevailing approach of the institution she is asked to serve. Cherniss (1976) notes that he has frequently "witnessed individuals who were committed to a 'radical-humanistic' concept of education assume the role of consultant" to a traditionally oriented school system. "In virtually every case I know of the consultation failed either with a 'bang' (the consultants were eventually asked to leave in no uncertain terms) or with a 'whimper' (the consultants—discouraged, hurt and frustrated—eventually left without a sense of accomplishment)" (p. 16). The consultant has the responsibility of making a decision as to the validity, feasibility, and appropriateness of the invitation. Merely passively allowing oneself to be chosen without actively involving oneself in the process of choice may ultimately make for an unproductive consultation experience.

The ruminations of a mental health center staff consultant who has been called in by a school administrator illustrate some of these postcontact, pre-entry problems. The principal is concerned about "problem" children in the school and asks the consultant to meet with him to discuss this. During the initial contact the principal indicates that he would like the consultant to set up "a group counseling or group treatment session for these particular children maybe once or twice a week."

On the way back to the office after meeting with the principal, the consultant asks himself the following questions:

1. Who's hurting? As far as I can tell, it's mainly the principal, and if he's right, also the teachers. I don't know the [school guidance] counselor's role in this yet and I really know very little about the children.

2. Why are they calling me now? The principal's last remark may be the most significant. He said a few teachers might quit, and he really seems pressured to do something. He wants to get the teachers off his back, maybe.

3. What is this current theory of the problem? It seems to be that it's mostly the children's fault. They probably do have some difficult children. But he also said Miss Taylor seems to have the most trouble and she's new. What about the way the other fifth and sixth grade teachers handle the problems? I should find out how he views the other teachers.

4. What might be camouflaged? Hard to say, but there might be a really big hassle between those teachers and the principal about some other things. The turnover rate is high, although not way out of line for city schools. It may be that overall morale is bad. There is

also some hint that the teachers are frustrated with their ineffectiveness in helping children read. And even though the [school
guidance] counselor had to fill in for another teacher, I don't think
that the principal had invited her to our meeting anyway; nor does it
sound as if he fully discussed it with her.

5. Is there a problem which could be helped by mental health
input? Perhaps. I'd want to know more. Certainly, I want to talk to
those other people. A group meeting with the teachers really might
give me a better idea.

6. Do I want to get involved with this school and what are my
personal priorities? I like the principal and have also heard that his
reputation is good. Unless I can be convinced, however, I really
don't want to work with the children in a group. I can do that kind
of thing back at the clinic. If I'm going to work in the school, I'd
rather work with school personnel than with the children. Maybe I
could help people in the school to help other children. I'd like to at
least go ahead and explore it with them.

7. What are my resources? If I work out a consultative program
here, I'll have to do it alone. No one in my agency has the time to
help me at this point. I don't like working alone but there is no
other choice now. At least, I have the time available. (Hetznecker
and Forman, 1974, pp. 69–70)

Entry and Associated Problems

The problem of entry is that of a stranger's accession to an
ongoing social system. The consultant is an outsider, and provision has to be made for his temporary incorporation into the
agency. Entry of the consultant threatens established relationships and patterns of interaction. Since the consultant is new
to the agency his behavior is relatively unpredictable (Glidewell,
1959). Entry is easiest for the consultant when his function is
sponsored and sanctioned by the highest administrative official
in the agency. Others in the agency are then constrained to be a
least favorably disposed to working with the consultant.

Savage (1952) found that one of the factors associated with success or failure in consultation was the agency administration's interest in, or hostility toward, consultation. Furthermore, if consultation has the acceptance of the administration, then the necessary steps may be taken to prepare the staff for the introduction of the consultant. This involves meetings with the staff to explain the utility and value of consultation, how the consultant might be used, the administrative procedures involved in requesting consultation, alleviating staff anxiety about consultation generally and about this consultant in particular.

A series of gatekeepers controls access to the organization and its personnel. The sanction of the administrator to the consultant's entry gives access to the organization; sanction by the supervisory staff gives access to task areas in the organization. Without such sanctions the consultant has no entitlement to access, to agency information, or to the agency's work force. The acceptance of consultation by these gatekeepers need to be obtained. And their acceptance needs to be obtained in crossing boundaries within the agency—from administrator to supervisor, from supervisor to worker. This, however, presents some problems at the point of contact and entry.

PROBLEMS FOR THE ADMINISTRATOR

The entry of the consultant presents problems at each level of the agency hierarchy—at the executive administrative level, at the middle-management supervisory level, and at the direct-service worker level.

The administrator may have some anxiety about the fact that a knowledgeable stranger will become aware of some of the deficiencies in agency operation. If the consultant is to do his work effectively, agency staff will have to share frankly with him something of the problems faced by the agency and the personnel. The family's dirty linen will have to be exposed. The administrator, who is perceived as representing the agency to the community, may be uneasy about such sharing and the implied evaluation of his leadership in the mind of the consultant. Agencies "like primitive tribes have rituals, taboos, social documents and the like" (Brown, 1967, p. 402) which need to be protected and shared only infrequently under special protected conditions. The administrator is likely to feel heightened anxiety in those instances in which the consultant represents a licensing authority, an accrediting group, or an administratively superior agency.

The resistance to consultation which derives from agency anxiety about sharing its deficiences with an "outsider" is particularly acute for newly developed agencies in ghetto areas in relation to a social work consultant. Roberts (1968) points out that social workers "are widely feared as competitors" with indigenous leaders "for control of programs . . . if weaknesses in their programs should be exposed by consultation, power might revert to the social work profession" (p. 340). The administrator has to make a decision "that the gains to be had from disclosing his [agency's weaknesses] to the consultant are greater than the gains to be had from concealment" (p. 341). Recently developed agencies funded by tenuous appropriations are in keen competition for scarce dollars. Any suggestion that the agency might not be fulfilling its mission might jeopardize its funding (Bonkowski, 1968).

Not only is there anxiety about exposure of deficiencies, there also is "status anxiety." Administrative staff of many new agencies have limited professional education, are anxious about their competence, and consequently are reluctant to engage in professional interaction where these shortcomings might become obviously apparent. If confidentiality, acceptance of, and respect for, the consultee are of prime importance in any consultation interaction they are of even greater significance in consultation with newly formed agencys headed by representatives of neighborhood groups.

PROBLEMS AT THE SUPERVISORY LEVEL
At the supervisory level anxiety about the introduction of the consultant may even be more acute. The supervisor has the ini-

tial responsibility for helping the worker with work-related problems. Consequently, consultation might frequently be perceived as potentially competitive. Consultant and supervisor share the worker for a time and are competing for the respect of the worker. The questions for the supervisor are: Can the consultant be more helpful than I am to the worker? Will he supersede me as a source of help? The consultant may be perceived as competing with the supervisor for a leadership role with the workers and for the affections and respect of the workers.

The supervisor also responds to the threat of the potential conflict between himself and the consultant instigated by the worker. The worker may attempt to use the professional authority of the consultant against the administrative authority of the supervisor. Consultation can thus become an instrument of rivalrous intrigue. The worker may raise the same question with both supervisor and consultant and, getting different answers, may confront the supervisor with this.

In being accepted into the system, the consultant becomes functionally a part of the system, at least temporarily. Any unilateral extension of his prerogatives, any attempt to usurp the responsibility or authority of others operating in the system, creates problems.

It does a disservice to the worker if the consultant disrupts the relationship between supervisor and worker. The worker is dependent on the continuing relationship with the supervisor for help and support and can only count on this from the consultant on an intermittent basis. The consultant thus has some responsibility to "support the administrative and structural relationships of the agency and to enhance the support mechanisms that the worker could get through his or her supervisor" (Hetznecker and Forman, 1974, p. 110).

Supervisors are in a key position to help workers resolve resistance to consultation. Maddux (1950) points out that:

Feeling mobilized in workers by psychiatric consultation was often expressed to the supervisors and the problem which supervisors

brought up most frequently in their conferences (with the consultant) was the management of worker anxiety and hostility toward the
psychiatrist or toward psychiatry in general. . . . The supervisor
was found to have a vital role in helping the workers to use consultation and in dealing with feeling mobilized in the worker by consultation. (pp. 763, 764)

Resolving workers' opposition to consultation is important
because while "the subordinate in the client system does not
usually have the option of rejecting consultation that has been
arranged for him, his resistance may be deviously expressed"
(Robins, 1964, p. 6). Above all, it argues for the advisability,
here as elsewhere, of introducing a new element in the system
only after full discussion with, and acceptance by, the administrative and direct-service staff.

As a consequence of the distinct threat which consultation
often poses for supervisors there is some discussion as to
whether or not supervisors should be included in consultation
sessions requested by their workers. Haylett and Rapoport
(1964) note that with the introduction of a consultant,

anxiety and disequilibrium are particularly marked in the intermediate echelons, among supervisors. . . . This may be attributed to the
fact that the consultant's role and function does have some elements
in common with other staff development methods. . . . For this
reason during the initial contacts we prefer to invite the supervisory
staff to attend consultation sessions with subordinates. (p. 335)

One social work consultant, recognizing that the presence
of the supervisor might inhibit the consultee, nevertheless concludes that "it is advantageous for the first time supervisor to be
present. Since the consultant is in no way responsible for the
performance of the social worker it might prove disastrous if the
worker, on the basis of discussion with the consultant, carried
out a decision contrary to the thinking of the supervisor or the
policy of the agency" (May, 1970, p. 153).

Kaufman (1956) contends that "consultation with a case-worker, where the supervisor is present, achieves maximum usefulness" (p. 227). Since the supervisor will have continuing responsibility for helping the worker with the problem situation after the consultant leaves, it would be helpful if he were familiar with what actually was covered during the consulting session. It diminishes the possibility of the development of the triangular, competitive, rivalrous relationship referred to above in which the consultee plays off the consultant against the supervisor. As a participant in the consultation the supervisor can explain his point of view. The actual presence of the supervisor prevents the displacement of the supervisor by the consultant and reduces the likelihood of usurpation of the supervisor's function.

While presence of the supervisor may inhibit the supervisee-consultee, while it may risk competition between supervisor and consultant, while it may lead to diffusion of authority vis-à-vis the supervisee-consultee, it has the advantages cited above as well as others. It may enable the consultant to improve communication between supervisor and supervisee, it makes available, in the supervisor, a resource person who is familiar with agency policy and who can help to sort out those solutions which are both feasible and congruent with agency procedures. Above all, it may make supervisors more comfortable about consultation, since it may reassure them that threats to their position are more imagined than real. Where it is appropriate, an invitation to participate in the consultation with the worker might be extended to the supervisor with the recognition that he might very well refuse.

Some suggest that while it is desirable for supervisors to participate in consultation conferences when this is a new procedure in the agency the necessity diminishes as the staff develops more experience with consultation (Insley 1959, p. 223). However it is done, reducing the sense of threat and concomitant anxiety which consultation poses for supervisors is crucial. This is because the response of the direct-service worker to consultation is conditioned, to some extent, by the supervisor's attitude. A study which reviewed the use of peer consultation by public assistance personnel noted that "workers who perceived that their supervisors held favorable attitudes toward their problem-solving interchanges with their peers tended to originate consultation more often than did those who perceived their supervisors as holding negative attitudes" (Anderson and Carlsen, 1972, p. 23). While the study was concerned with peer consultation, the results would seem applicable to the general use of consultation.

The report of a special project offering consultation to workers in a public child welfare agency notes that the "consultant-supervisor relationship is the strategic area in the consultation program. The supervisor is the key person who deals with all important issues relating to consultation" (Rosenthal and Sullivan, 1959, p. 23).

The supervisor-consultant relationship involves many questions of procedure and ethics. An ethical question around confidentiality is sometimes posed. Inevitably, the consultant makes some assessment of the consultee's competence as he becomes familiar with his work. How does she handle a request from the consultee's supervisor that the consultant share his opinion of the consultee's competence with the supervisor? If the consultation contract anticipates this question by spelling out clearly that the consultant will not disclose anything that goes on in the consultation conference with others on the staff, she can justifiably withhold his assessment. However, does not the inclusion of such an understanding in the consultation contract increase the supervisor's anxiety and intensify his resistance to the whole idea of consultation? On the other hand, would not a failure to recognize clearly the consultee's rights to confidentiality inhibit his frank participation in the consultation—particularly if the consultee feels that some component of the work problem he wants to discuss is related to his supervisor and to agency policy? The consultant might accept the responsibility for helping to free communication between worker and supervisor and worker and administration. Alternatively, she might invite the consultee to participate in any conference he has with the supervisor regarding consultation sessions that involve the consultee.

There is some reality to the fear that the consultant is being used as a channel for communication of confidential information. Robins (1964) notes that in his experience:

> Various levels in the hierarchy represented by the [consulted] system may try to make use of the consultant in obtaining information denied to them as a result of their function in the hierarchy. This works both ways, that is, the lower levels in the client system may want to know what is going on at the top and the top may want to know what is going on at the bottom. (p. 7)

These are some of the problems which entry of the consultant into the social system of the agency poses for supervisory staff.

PROBLEMS FOR THE DIRECT-SERVICE STAFF

For the direct-service worker, introduction of the consultant poses a threat to professional narcissism and anxiety about change. In requesting the help of the consultant the worker makes a public admission of his failure to handle a work-related problem.

In an interview study of thirty-nine consultees, Macarov (1968) found that consultees manifested problems in asking for help and tended to disguise their request for help. Thus consultees viewed

> the activity which consultants termed giving advice as that of receiving information—whereas consultants saw themselves as advisors, consultees tended to see them to a larger degree as resource persons. . . . Some consultees denied receiving help from the consultants or minimized the amount received while being highly favorable to the process used, the results obtained and their willingness to call upon the consultants again. (p. 6)

There is resistance to change here as elsewhere, and the consultee may face some reluctance to engage in consultation because it may involve the necessity for changing his approach, changing his way of working, modifying his thinking. There is a concern about whom the consultant represents, and her ties to the administrative establishment. While she comes, as we have noted, without any administrative authority, the consultant nevertheless does represent the administration of the agency, and this is likely to create some anxiety on the part of the consultee. He might perceive the supervisor and administrator as "spying" on his behavior via the consultant. Here, once again, the desirability of some understanding about the confidentiality of the consultant relationship needs to be clearly established and accepted by participants.

At the very least the use of consultation might require some additional work on the part of the consultee in preparing material for the consultation. Consultation is an imposition on his time and energy. Direct-service workers may resent the fact that they have the least power to resist the mandate from agency administration that consultation be utilized (Mann, 1972).

Neither the individual social agency client nor the individual social agency worker has the prerogative of selecting the person with whom they would prefer to work. The consultant is a given which the worker has no choice but to accept if she wants consultation. It has been suggested that a panel of consultants might be made available so that the worker can have a choice.

For both the supervisor and the direct-service worker the entry of the consultant is made more acceptable, less threatening, when it is clear that the expertise of the consultant is clearly and distinctively different from that which either the supervisor and/or the worker are supposed to possess.

As Bergen says, "the professional self-image is not jeopardized when he can declare that what he is lacking is something he need not (or should not) be expected to have in the first place, such as a specialized knowledge or technical capability" outside his area of competence or expertise (Bergen *et al.*, 1970, p. 399). For the worker the request for help is not demeaning; for the supervisor the consultant's offer of help to the worker is not competitive.

In many consultative situations this condition does obtain. This generally involves a member of one profession, having one body of knowledge for which he is held responsible, consulting with a member of another profession who possesses different knowledge and skills—psychiatrist and social worker, psychologist and nurse, lawyer and psychiatrist, social worker and teacher. There is a frequent, similar situation in those instances in which both consultant and consultee are members of the same profession but are affiliated with clearly different subspecialties—medical social worker and school social worker, psychiatrist and surgeon, mechanical engineer and electrical engineer. In all of these situations the consultee and the consultee organization can feel comfortable in asking for the consultant's help because they are "excused" from the responsibility of knowing what the consultant knows. They can take solace in Mark Twain's dictum: "We are all ignorant, we're just ignorant about different things." The more contiguous, more similar two professions are in terms of functions performed and techniques used, the greater the actuality of threat of competitive usurpation of roles. Similarity in function and procedures increases the problems of consultation between two professions. The consultee wonders what the consultant knows that he also has the responsibility for knowing but does not know. The anxiety for the consultant is intensified as he wonders about what he knows that the consultee does not know. The easiest consultation is between professionals who share very little in common in terms of function and expertise.

Some of this is made clear in a study by Griffith and Libo (1968) which points to the different levels of receptivity to mental health consultation they encountered in establishing a statewide program of consultation in New Mexico. Teachers and public health nurses were more receptive than physicians in private practice, and local welfare departments were ambivalent. "Some of the opposition stemmed from negative attitudes held by social work professionals in the high ranks of welfare department organization—they believed the mental health consultation program duplicated services already offered by their department" (p. 147).

CONSULTANT'S PROBLEMS

The acceptance of a consultation assignment also poses problems for the consultant. Coming as a stranger he is uncertain about the reception he may receive. He may be welcomed as a guest or resented as an intruder. He is uneasy about the fact that while those with whom he will be working know each other and are familiar with the agency, its operations, procedures, traditions, formal and informal structure, he himself is a stranger in a strange land. This unfamiliarity is discomforting and disconcerting. He is aware that, at least initially, his expertise is open to question and to testing. Will he, in fact, be able to be helpful to the consultee and the consultee organization? The consultant is more keenly aware of the limits of his expertise than are the others, and while they may be skeptical about his ability to help, he himself is, perhaps, even more uneasy about this. At the same time, he feels keenly his obligation to be of help, particularly if he is being paid for the consultation. Such feelings may present a problem.

> Since the consultant knows that he is expected to contribute something that his client lacks he is likely to feel considerable obligation to be of value—anxiety about demonstrating his value can stimulate him to rush forward prematurely with information or suggestions. His major concern becomes that of impressing his client rather than serving him. (Charters, 1956, p. 43)

The consultant's anxiety about her ability to be helpful also may be intensified by the recognition that often the most dif-

ficult cases, the most difficult situations, are selected for consultation. These problems come to consultation because nobody has
been able to find a viable solution. Hence the challenge is likely
to be great.

The consultant recognizes that she is both wanted and resented by the consultee—as is true for all with whom we have a
relationship of dependency. The ambivalent response that the
consultant can anticipate from the consultee is exemplified by
the sign on one consultant's door: "Socrates was a man who went
about counseling and advising people. They poisoned Socrates."
Similarly, an astute statesman once noted that there were three
principal ways for a politician to ruin his career—chasing
women, gambling, and trusting experts. Women were most
pleasurable, gambling was quickest, but trusting experts was the
surest way. Covert hostility is also apparent in the frequently
repeated quip that a consultant is "a drip under pressure."

The consultant often operates in a context which provokes
anxiety because it is bereft of some supportive elements. A consultant often "operates away from his home base in a social system in which he is only temporarily and tangentially affiliated.
There is little structure in which to operate, except what he
creates, and there is not the usual supporting framework to
which he is accustomed" (Rapoport, 1963, p. 15). The ambivalence is exemplified by the contrasting roles in which the
consultant may be perceived by agency personnel. The consultants may be seen as allies or community agents by administrators, as competitors or collaborators by supervisors, as spies or
saviors by workers.

The consultant has the problem of controlling some very
human reactions to situations frequently encountered. While he
should be confident of the help he can offer he should be equally
capable of sharing his limitations. He needs to resist seduction
into omniscience, which is one of the occupational hazards of
consultation (Stringer, 1961). Isaiah's admonition is pertinent:
"Woe unto them who are wise in their own eyes." The narcissistic desire of the consultant to present himself as an expert is

reinforced by the desire of the consultee to have available a resource from which can flow all answers to all questions.

Knowing some of the answers, the consultant must resist the temptation to believe he has all of the answers; that he is the all-knowing oracle the staff hopes he is. He needs to be able to counter the feelings of resentment and narcissistic hurt which are likely to be generated by any rejection of his suggestions and advice. He needs to be able to resist feeling apologetic about the fact that he is, in this instance, a "sayer" and the consultee is a "doer." The consultant talks about problems, but the consultee has the responsibility for taking action, for doing something about the problems. The consultant may feel derogated by the consultee whom he senses might be thinking that it is easy to talk but difficult to act. He needs to be able to accept the fact that others will receive credit for achievements which derive from his suggestions and advice while he himself may be denied recognition.

The consultant, paid by the agency, is in an ambiguous, marginal situation. "He is of the agency but not entirely in it." (Boehm, 1956, p. 246). He is not as fully bound by agency procedures, dictates, or tradition as are other staff members. This freedom from agency constraints enforced on other staff, his schedule which permits him to come and go, is an advantage which may be resented by the rest of the staff.

These are some of the problems faced by the principal actors in the consultation drama—administrator, supervisor, worker, consultant—and activated by the entry of the consultant.

Consultation Contracts

Some of the problems associated with entry of the consultant can be prevented or mitigated by a clearly defined contract. As in supervision, the consultative relationship operates best when there is a clear understanding between the participants as to the nature of reciprocal roles, obligations, and expectations. The structure of service needs to be clearly defined, understood, and accepted. The details of these understandings is embodied in a consultation "contract." This might be formally or informally arrived at, informally or formally formulated. What is involved in such a "contract" is a mutual agreement on the essential details of how the consultant, the consultee agency, and the individual consultees will be working together. The "contract" includes details regarding the following essentials: the functions the consultant will perform; the consultees with whom, and for whom, such functions will be performed; how much time the consultant will give, and how frequently such meetings will be held; what remuneration the consultant will receive; where consultation sessions will be held; what kinds of material the consultee organization and the individual consultee will provide in preparation for the consultation; what use the consultant will make of the information provided; with whom, and under what conditions, the consultant will share information about what goes on in the consultation session; what procedures are to be used in consultation; the objectives of consultation and the identified criteria which will enable participants to know if the objectives have been achieved; the consultant's obligations for evaluation and follow-up.

The "contract" involves structural, procedural, and psychological aspects. Discussion of contract specifications is not unlike the intake process in social work. Two strangers are coming together to participate jointly in a complex undertaking and they need to establish mutual agreements about the structure and conditions in accordance with which they will be working. And, as in intake, the "contract" is renegotiated, redefined, and revised as the participants work together and get a clearer, more precise idea of the working agreement they negotiated (Gebbie, 1970). During the contract negotiation period consultant and consultee agency get to know each other and begin to develop a sense of trust in each other.

Formulating a contract has the advantage of clarifying and making explicit the expectations held by consultants and consultees. It needs to be recognized that very often consultation takes place at the interface between two systems—the school system and the community mental health system, the nursing home system and the social service system, the social agency system and the legal system. Even the in-house consultant operates at the point of interface—in this case, at the interface between two units in the organization. The social work consultant representing the social service department in the hospital may meet with a nursing consultee who represents the nursing unit on the floor. A consultant from the group home unit of the agency may meet with a consultee working in the foster care unit. Entry-contracting negotiations are efforts to mesh effectively the gears of the two systems as they engage with one another. Ambiguity in expectations, as well as differences in expectations, can make for difficulties in the ongoing relationship. Mann (1973) found that ambiguity in the definition of the consultant's role was likely to be associated with less effective consultation experiences. Congruences in consultee-consultant expectations were associated with a higher perception of the usefulness of the consultation by consultees (p. 190).

Timing for contracting may be important. Contracts may be formulated before the consultee is ready for such a procedure. He may have only a vague, indefinite knowledge about the nature of consultation, the procedures, and expectations associated with it. By the time he knows what needs to be known, a contract is not really necessary since a mutually acceptable informal agreement may have developed.

Despite the desirability of an explicit contract, an empirical study of consultation arrangements shows that "vague agreements presumed to be in existence by both participants but never verbalized in any detail are by far the most common"

(MacClung and Stunden, 1970, p. 36). However, 76 percent of the respondents in the questionnaire survey (Kadushin and Buckman, 1977) indicated that while they did not generally formulate a written contract with the consultee there was, in the greatest percentage of such cases, an informal agreement of understanding in lieu of such a contract. Items in either the formal contract or informal understanding generally included, in descending order of frequency:

1. The purpose of the scheduled consultations(s)
2. The specific functions expected of the consultant
3. The specific individuals or groups designated as consultees
4. Frequency of scheduled consultations
5. Location of the consultation meeting
6. Nature of written reports required of consultant
7. Materials to be made available in preparation for consultation
8. Arrangements for follow-up evaluation
9. Confidentiality of material shared with consultant by the consultee
10. Fee for scheduled consultation.

As a component of the contract negotiation stage in the consultation process, agency administration has the responsibility for establishing clearly defined procedures so that the staff understands who can request consultation and the conditions under which the request can be made. The mechanics for consultation need to be spelled out by the administration. This includes requirements regarding preparation of material for a consultation, provision of time and secretarial help in preparation, responsibility for scheduling, and so forth. Agency administration has the further responsibility for helping the staff accept the value and rationale of consultation, the objective it is designed to achieve, the contribution it can make to agency service. This is in terms of ensuring attitudinal acceptance of consultation. The "contract" provides the basis for interpretation to the staff about the details of consultation.

Just as agency administration has the responsibility of preparing staff for the introduction of the consultant to the agency, it has the further responsibility of introducing the agency to the consultant. Agency administration orients the consultant to the agency purpose, objectives, and procedures. The administrator makes material available and answers questions the consultant may have. In contact and contract negotiations something as simple as parking facilities for the consultant and an assigned room for the consultation may be easily overlooked.

Preparation for introduction of the consultant might include a period of orientation and observation in the agency. This would include an opportunity to talk with, and ask questions of, members of the staff and to observe what can be observed of the actual functioning of the agency.

The agency, in arranging for consultation, has to assess the cost involved in the expenditure of staff time. Not only is it necessary to release time so that consultees can prepare for, and participate in, consultation, it is also important that consultees, supervisors, and consultant have time to meet with each other, get to know and understand each other (Rosenthal and Sullivan, 1959, pp. 24–26).

Summary

The various ways of making contact between consultant and consulted were reviewed, some consideration being given to the difference between voluntary and not-so-voluntary consultation. The different motives for consultation were outlined as well as the problems encountered by consultants and consultees, as a consequence of consultation. The nature of consultation contracts and content was discussed. The chapter was concerned with the steps in the process leading up to the consultation interaction.

Chapter Five

The Consultation Process:
Preparing, Beginning,
Working Through, Terminating

The sequential steps in the process discussed in the previous chapter all serve to pave the way for beginning a specific consultation event. We are now at that point in the process where a consultant, having been contacted, and granted entry to the agency on some explicit contractual terms, is ready to provide consultation to some designated consultee representing the agency and its service.

Preparing and Beginning
by the Consultee

Like all processes, consultation begins before it starts in the preparation engaged by both consultant and consultee. We noted above that some of the preliminary preparation is accomplished during the contract negotiation phase. The consultant becomes generally acquainted with the agency and the agency with the consultant. However, for each consultation incident, specific and relevant preparation is necessary.

Workers need to be able to recognize a problem in their work which is perceived as the responsibility of the profession represented by the consultant. Unless the prospective consultee can clearly make such an identification, it is not likely that she will be able to use consultation appropriately. Fogelson (1970) points to this as a problem in the use of legal consultation by social workers. In interviews with social workers, they were presented

> with a series of situations culled from the analyzed cases. They were asked to identify the legal component (if any) and to indicate whether they thought legal consultation or referral was necessary. Responses were varied and often unrelated to the reality of the legal situation. The workers were then asked: "Suppose, over a period of several weeks, a client complained to you that a strange lump on her back was growing larger. In addition, she seemed to be doing nothing about it. What would you, as the worker do?" Almost all workers responded similarly: a quizzical look, a pause, and then (often accompanied by laughter) the comment, "I'd see to it that she saw a doctor." The analogy between the medical and legal referral was quite clear. Why the distinction between the reactions to the two situations? Perhaps one worker summed it up when she suggested that the reason referrals to lawyers were not made was that, in legal situations, we don't recognize the "lump." (p. 101)

The consultee needs to know enough about the kind of knowledge and skill that is likely to be possessed by a consultant with a given professional affiliation. If she knows nothing about psychiatry, it is not likely that she can intelligently make use of what a psychiatrist has to offer. This factor is of concern to social work. The ambiguous image which many other professions have of social work and the nature of social work expertise hampers their making effective preparation for social work consultation.

Not knowing clearly what social workers can do or can offer, they are uncertain about when social work consultation might be appropriate.

Clearly defining the problem helps to determine whether the consultant selected is the appropriate one. It would be unproductive to meet with a psychiatric consultant if the problem is primarily a legal one; it would be inappropriate to meet with a day care consultant if the problem is one of establishing foster care facilities.

Thinking through these kinds of questions will determine the focus and content of the consultation interaction. Additional preparation requires that the consultee clarify for himself the nature of his attitudes and feelings toward consultation generally and toward this consultant in particular.

On occasion the consultee may have had previous contact with the consultant which left him with residual positive or negative feelings which now intrude to shape initially the nature of his responses to this consultant.

If the consultant is a stranger she still comes bearing some professional title. The consultee may have feelings about the profession with which the consultant is affiliated. He may be grateful that he has the opportunity for professional contact with a psychiatrist, or he may be cynical about psychiatry in general and how much help it can offer anybody. Social workers' stereotyped perceptions of lawyers as "judgmental," "authoritarian," and "restricted in scope" may make them hesitant in using legal consultation even when it is perceived as appropriate (Fogelson, 1970); (see also Bell, 1975). The consultee social worker might feel himself superior to the consulting physiotherapist and wonder how much the consultant knows about anything consequential. The images the consultee has in his mind about the status relationship between the profession he represents and the profession the consultant represents act to contaminate the nature of the consultative interaction.

There is a need to be aware of fundamental differences in

orientation between some consultants and consultees—the
teacher's commitments to the group as against the caseworker's
commitments to the individual; the psychiatric social worker's
commitment to a clinical mental health orientation in understanding behavior, the policeman's commitments to a more
authoritarian-regulatory orientation to behavior. As Confucius
says, "those who follow different roads cannot take counsel with
one another."

The consultee, here as in supervision, needs to be aware of
his feelings about the age, sex, and racial differences between
himself and the consultant. Depending on the consultee's reactions to these factors he may act defensive, apologetic, deferen-
tial, submissive, superior, condescending, resistive, or patroniz-
ing. As he examines his feelings about the impending
consultation does the consultee feel ready to share freely with
the consultant, is he resistive to the whole idea of consultation,
does he feel demeaned by the necessity for consultation, does he
feel comfortable in communicating with the consultants his inability to resolve this problem without help, is he anxious about
self-exposure, and so on?

The fact is that a request for consultation triggers a series of
feeling reactions in the consultee. The consultation interaction
will go more smoothly if, in preparation, the consultee attempts
some introspective self-analysis so that he can be more explicitly
aware of the feelings he is bringing into the interaction in which
he is scheduled to participate.

The consultee needs to define, as clearly as possible, the
problem or situation with which he wants help, the nature of the
help he hopes to obtain from the consultant, and the specific
ways in which he thinks the consultant can be helpful. In preparing for the consultation, and as an aid to the consultant in
preparing for the consultation, the consultee should formulate a
request for consultation which includes a statement of the general problem and the specific questions the consultee wants clarified. Some agencies have formulated a consultation outline
which serves as an aid in structuring the consultation request.

Formally organizing the material for presentation, here as in the case of supervision, gives the "worker the opportunity to organize his thinking on the [problem] and to focus on those areas where he especially wants discussion. This procedure helps to prevent the floundering which is common to the initial, more anxious period and which when it occurs tends to increase the general anxiety and diminish the effectiveness of consultation" (Kaufman, 1956, p. 226).

It is recognized that consultees see preparation of summaries for consultation as time-consuming. In agencies with heavy caseloads such a requirement may not only be resisted, it may in fact be infeasible (Rosenthal and Sullivan, 1959, p. 11). Time and effort constraints not only present difficulties for adequate preparation for consultation, they make for difficulty in scheduling consultation meetings. Thus, working in a public school setting and finding times when teachers are available for a conference can be problematic if the consultee really does not want to stay late, come early, or give up lunch. Effective use of consultation may require that the administrator make substitute time available to relieve the teacher who has a consultation conference scheduled.

Consultation is, for the consultee, a secondary activity. Teaching, social working, administering, and so on, is the primary task of the consultee and one which is given priority. To find time for consultation means a temporary detour from primary tasks.

Rosenthal and Sullivan (1959) noted this as a factor in the workers' opposition to consultation:

It was my impression that such participation as came from the child welfare workers pointed to a not-too-eager acceptance of anything new that might add to the many existing work pressures. One or two of the less guarded workers raised such questions as: What exactly in the way of extra work would this means for me? Another wanted to know where he was going to get time to come to consultation. (p. 16)

The supervisor can contribute to the success of the consultation by helping the supervisee to accept and adequately prepare for the consultation conference.

Preparing and Beginning by the Consultant

Consultant preparation parallels consultee preparation. The consultant needs to review her general knowledge of the agency shared with her during the contract negotiation phase. She should reacquaint herself with the functions, structure, and services of the agency so that she can better understand the question(s) posed for her by the consultee. She needs to read and think about the material forwarded to her in advance by the consultee relevant to this particular consultation. She might review the literature and research relevant to the scheduled consultation and review her previous experience with similar problems. She might select pertinent material such as articles, research instruments and reports, forms, and so forth, to take to the meeting.

But the consultant also has feelings and attitudes about consultation generally, about consultation with this kind of agency in particular, and specifically about what is being asked of her in this consultation. Does she really feel confident that she can be of any help? Does she feel that the specialized knowledge and skills she brings to the consultation are adequate to the demands she is likely to encounter? Does she feel that the agency service is ineffective, and its' workers inadequately prepared to use anything she might have to offer, or does she feel that the objectives of the agency are significant and important and the staff capable of implementing its' mission?

Not only might the consultant have some feeling about the professional designation of the consultee, she may also have feelings about the institution to which she is asked to consult. She might regard the school system as repressive and archaic, the courts as selectively punitive instruments of social control, the day care center system as inimical to the stability of the American family.

Similarly, the consultant needs to clarify for herself her own hidden agenda. For instance, a consultant might view "schools as being too rigid, too inflexible or too authoritarian. She might agree on a verbal level to help teachers understand the children better; however on the emotional level her attitude is to go in there and soften up those rigid inflexible teachers" (Berkowitz, 1975, p. 41). Being aware of his hidden agenda may enable the consultant to prepare for her consultation somewhat differently.

Consultants might approach the system with the attitude that its administration is apt to be conservative and opposed to change and that in response to this the administration has to be "avoided, worked around or even overcome" by developing support among the workers for innovative changes. It might be noted parenthetically that a detailed study of consultation to schools concludes, however, that "no single course can kill a good program more rapidly. No administrator wants people in his organization who are working at purposes contrary to his own. When he suspects this he will quickly terminate the program or greatly curtail its impact" (Behavior Science Corporation, 1973, p. 89).

Another question which needs to be considered in achieving clarity in the experience for both consultant and consultee is the "constituency issue." Does the consultant see herself as primarily serving the interests and needs of the agency, the staff, the client group, the community which provides the funds for agency support? The traditional rhetorical response to the issue is that serving the need of one constituency is to serve the needs of others—that what is good for the staff is good for the agency, is good for the clients. This, however, ignores the fact that there might, on occasion, be conflicts of interest. The consultant needs to clarify for herself, in preparation for the consultation, the constituency group to which she is giving priority (Cherniss, 1976).

Once again, here is a complex of feelings which might be brought into the interaction, in this instance by the consultant, which would be less negatively intrusive if the consultant were aware of them. The success of consultation depends, in part, on the ability of the consultant to communicate an attitude of respect for the consultee's profession as well as for the consultee as a person. It needs to be noted that a consultant from "any field must be able to recognize and be willing to respect the primacy of the field to which he is lending knowledge. No matter how important and useful in his own field, as a consultant he plays a supplementary role to another profession" (Garrett, 1956, p. 234). However, concomitant with respect for the consultee and a readiness to affirm the knowledge and expertise of the consultee and his profession is an attitude of respect for the real difference between them. They are equal as people but different in the expertise which they bring to the situation which engages their attention, the consultant being more expert than the consultee.

Both consultee and consultant need some commonality in points of view about the phenomena with which they are jointly concerned. Psychiatrists oriented in terms of an orthodox Freudian framework find difficulty in consulting currently with public welfare social workers who tend, frequently, to be oriented in terms of an environmental determinism model of psychosocial distress. Not only do consultant and consultee lack a common frame of reference, they hold conflicting frames of reference.

Basing his comments on the experience developed through a special project in which research consultation was offered to social agencies, Warren (1963) writes of the difficulties in consultation which resulted from differences between the subculture of the practitioner and the subculture of the researcher, differences which had not been clearly identified in preparation for the consultation. These differences in their orientation to research held by the consultant and consultee hindered effective implementation of the process of consultation.

In preparing for a consultation visit consideration needs to be given to determining with some precision who is the target of consultation. A distinction may be made between the "person initiating the request" and the "real consultee."

If the consultant himself is given the opportunity and sanction of selecting the targets of consultation, it is suggested that he select those who bring greatest potential for impact on achieving the consultation objective. If the primary, immediate objective is client change, then those workers who have direct access to the client and greatest influence on the client are selected as the targets for consultation. If the objective is system change, then the target selected would more expeditiously be those administrators who have greatest power in the system. It is also suggested that the consultant make some assessment of the change potential of the various targets of choice with the aim of selecting that professional or that group of professionals in the system who are most amenable to change. All of this is nice and desirable but not easily done, if it can be done at all. Consultants have limited control in selecting the target of consultation and most often have to work with those who are available, accessible, and agreeable to acting in the role of consultee.

Preparation for actively engaging in consultation may involve informal procedures for getting acquainted with prospective consultees. Going to lunch with consultee agency workers, attending some of the routinely scheduled meetings, participating in their ceremonials, such as birthday celebrations, helps the consultant prepare for consultation. These activities reduce the social-emotional distance between consultant and consultee, make him more accessible and acceptable, and are part of the process of familiarization. Adapting Parker's (1968) comments, which in the original related to psychiatrists, one can say that "sterotyped ideas about [social workers] are still prevalent enough to warrant dissipating them by some degree of social contact if the occasion arises naturally."

These kinds of contacts, however, raise the danger that the consultant may develop personal relationships with consultees which militate against effective consultation and the danger that the consultant may be co-opted by some particular consultee clique.

In client-centered consultation, the consultant may wish to consider meeting with or observing the client in preparation for consultation (Bettleheim 1958; Brown 1966). The consultant may choose to sit in on the class in which the student of the consultee-teacher is a member or briefly interview the social worker-consultee's client.

The social work consultant not only needs to understand the culture of the consultee agency or organization, he has to prepare to accept and respect the priority given to the principal mission of that agency or organization. The principal mission of the school system is education; the principal mission of the court system is the legal response to crime and delinquency; the principal mission of the day care center is child care and education; the principal mission of the hospital is the cure of illness. In each case the principal concerns of social work are secondary and of interest to the consultee agency only and solely as they contribute to the implementation of its own primary mission. The social work consultant is not being asked to help the consultee implement social work aims and objectives but rather to help the consultee use her own expert knowledge and skills more effectively in implementation of her own particular, unique, professional responsibilities.

It may be for this reason that the more effective consultants are those who have worked in the system to which they are offering consultation, are intimately familiar with how the system operates, and are perceived by the consultees as knowing what it is like to be on the inside. Consultants who "have personal experience with the situation faced by their consultees . . . are less likely to be perceived as alien by the consultees and are more likely to prescribe recommendations which are directly relevant to the consultee's dilemma" (Behavior Science Corporation, 1973, p. 144). Such a background of familiar experiences also makes it easier for the consultant to establish his credibility with the consultee.

It might be noted further that in the same study of consultation to schools the perceived relevance of the consultant's help was associated with the extent to which consultees rated the consultation service as "exemplary," "average," or "nonexemplary."

> In every consultation program rated as highly effective, the consulting staff is providing help to the schools in such areas as classroom management and learning disabilities. . . . Involvements in these areas provide consultees with immediate positive results. One of the benefits of the approach is that consultees gain confidence in themselves and in their consultants. When this happens the consultative process blossoms. (Bheavior Science Corporation, 1973, p. 137)

Since the primary commitment of the consultee organization is to its own professional function, it is not unexpected that a study of the impact of mental health consultation to public school teachers noted that when asked what they feel should be the focus of their consultation,

> 74 percent of the consultees report that these sessions should focus "a great deal" on behavior problems in the classrooms; and 54 percent respond that they should focus "a greal deal" on learning difficulties (multiple answers were coded, adding to more than 100 percent). School administrators were asked what should be used as criteria for judging the success of school consultation problems. Management of classroom behavior problems and academic performance were the most popular choices (mentioned spontaneously by 48 percent of these respondents). The most pressing concern of the

schools is the educational process. . . . Their basic question to the consultants often implied but not stated is "Do you have skills that I can use?" (Plog, 1974, pp. 59–60)

Some 265 consultees, teachers and school administrators, were interviewed in this study. One principal-consultee said:

If the [community mental health] center is going to show its effectiveness, it needs to show how consultation has helped change behavior—how a naughty boy became good, a child who couldn't sit still in school and now can.

Another principal in another study notes that the consultants

are concerned about different things than I am. They worry about "thumbsuckers" and "bedwetters." What a kid does at home is none of my business. My problems are the kids who tear up the classrooms, start fires in the bathrooms, and threaten people with razor blades. As long as a kid doesn't cause problems at school, he can suck his thumb all he wants. (Behavior Science Corporation, 1973, p. 96)

If these attitudes seem to suggest a limited, narrow orientation to consultation on the part of these representatives of the school system, they nevertheless have to be respected as the expressed needs from consultation as perceived by these consultees.

The point of view does present a real dilemma for mental health consultants. If the basic rationale of mental health consultation to schools is to press the system to perform primary and secondary mental health prevention functions, the more exclusive concern of the system with its primary educative tasks diminishes the likelihood of achieving this objective. The mental health consultant, in order to be accepted in the performance of the functions that school personnel want from him, would, at least initially, have to be concerned primarily, if not exclusively, with mental health only as it affects education.

While presenting consultants with a dilemma, the experiential and resource data regarding consultation indicate that a sensitive awareness, understanding, and acceptance on the part of the consultants of the situation as seen by the consultees of the systems context in which the consultee carries on his work are indispensable prerequisites for effective consultation (see Reppucci *et al.*, 1973).

Interviews with mental health consultants about their work indicate that some are opposed to preparatory planning for their consultation conferences such as suggested here. The opposition derives from what these consultants regard as the desirable approach to consultation. In reporting the results of such interviews with consultants (Behavior Science Corporation, 1973), the researchers note that nondirectively oriented consultants

express concerns about "creating an atmosphere in which their consultees can experience personal growth," and about "not imposing their own ideas on their consultees." They are likely to operate on an ad lib basis—that is, they just show up for a consultation appointment without any preconception of what the topic of discussion will be. The following comments, taken from some of these consultants, typify this approach.

"I don't think you can be successful in the schools if you impose your ideas or values on them [consultees]. I don't tell my consultees what to talk about and I try not to contaminate the outcome with my ideas. I let them talk about what they want to. I don't make recommendations to them about what to do with a child. I figure they know a lot more about the kid and the school than I do. If you set a climate where they can talk, they'll find their own answers to their problems."

"I don't prepare any type of presentation before I meet with them [consultees]. I tried that a few times and it didn't matter any-

way. I always ask them at the beginning of the appointment what
they want to talk about and it is always different from what I prepared—so I quit preparing. It's important to talk about what they
want to talk about."

However, the interviews with consultees revealed that

> many consultees are not sophisticated enough in mental health and
> in the consultative process that they understand what the consultant
> expects of them. They often don't know what their problems are
> and, therefore, can't generate meaningful questions about them.
> What frequently happens is that they will talk about the first thing
> that comes to mind, whether it is relevant or not. Unfortunately,
> they frequently report that their sessions are not very worthwhile.
> This is a particularly common reaction to group consultation where
> the consultant takes an extremely non-directive approach. The truly
> unfortunate thing is that he reports that he is responding to his con-
> sultee's interests, yet he doesn't realize that he is wasting valuable
> opportunities to share with his consultees his own mental health tal-
> ents rather than expecting theirs to spring forth spontaneously from
> the unstructured climate he has nurtured. (pp. 94–95)

Some preparation for beginning may therefore be desirable
if not absolutely essential. While the consultant should keep her
options open and fluid, subject to reformulation in response to
the consultee's expressed needs and preferences, it would be
wise for the consultant to recognize explicitly that she does have
some initial predisposition as to how she defines her role and
how she plans to proceed. Recognition of the choices which
need to be made, the questions which need to be answered, and
an awareness on the part of the consultant with regard to where
she stands initially on these issues make the difference between
desirable flexibility and undesirable confusion and ambiguity.

Working Through

PRELIMINARY EXPOSITIONAL PHASE

All of this preparation takes place before the participants in the consultation actually meet. At some point, however, the consultant and the consultee actually get together and the interpersonal interaction actually begins.

Because, unlike supervision, which involves an ongoing relationship, the consultation conference is often engaged in by people who are strangers to each other, time at the beginning of the conference needs to be allocated to getting acquainted. An initial period of social interchange may help the participants make some initial appraisal of each other before formal assumption of the roles of consultee and consultant and the initiation of the formal consultation.

The initial phase of the interaction sets the stage for establishing the relationship and hence is of considerable importance. The report of a consultation project in a public child welfare agency notes that, "the experience with the project supports the belief that the initial stage of consultation is both the most crucial and the most difficult" (Rosenthal and Sullivan 1959, p. 15).

Studies of the actual consultation interaction indicate that the early period in interaction is concerned primarily with exposition (Mannino, 1972; Robbins and Spencer, 1968). The responsibility for task performance rests primarily with the consultee at this point. He presents a description of the problem, he offers information which would help the consultant understand the problem. Studying the tape recording of consultation sessions Robbins and Spencer (1968) conclude that,

> during the early part of the conference the client [consultee] talks for fairly long periods of time merely giving out information. The consultant listens, asking questions, giving information and reinforc-

ing the client. The initial phase of the meeting thus appears to be
expositional in nature in which the client's principal function is carried out. (p. 367)

The consultant's activity at this point is primarily internal. Lis-
tening carefully, he draws inference, develops diagnostic hypotheses, attempts to get a clear, accurate picture of the problem.

These differences in function are reflected in differences in
talk time during the preliminary period. "In the beginning of the
conference the [consultee] talked more and in considerably
greater amounts than the consultant. The length of the [consul-
tee's] average speech during the first fifth of a conference is
three to four times greater than that of the consultant's." The
consultant has to restrain himself and listen rather than react
prematurely. As Cook (1970) says in offering ten commandments
of consultation, "Thou shalt possess thy soul in patience and
avoid the trap of precipitance" (p. 305).

During this phase, too, the consultant attempts to help the
consultee define the problem in a manner which is congruent
with the expertise of the consultant. This might be done either
by reformulating the problem or by selective emphasis on some
particular aspects of the problem. The consultant's aim is to
translate the consultee's problem in a way which makes it amenable to the kind of expertise the consultant can offer. Too great
an incongruence may make it untranslatable into any "language"
the consultant knows. The responsible consultant would suggest
a referral to a more likely consultant at this point.

When the consultee is not clear as to the nature of his
problem and needs help in defining it, the consultant may be
more active—asking pertinent questions, reflecting, clarifying,
gently pointing to omissions, inconsistencies, and conflicts in the
consultee's presentation, eliciting further details and information. In all of this the consultant is concerned with learning not

only the nature of the problem per se but the consultee's feelings about the problem.

Here, as in supervision and in work with the client, what questions are asked and how they are asked is important. Questions which are phrased challengingly, questions which ask for information the consultee is not likely to have, questions which throw an undue responsibility and burden on the consultee for conducting the consultation conference are apt to evoke anxiety and increase resistance.

It may sound arrogant, but nevertheless it is true that defining the problem may be complicated by the fact that the consultee often erroneously believes she knows exactly what it is. It may be that she sees the problem from a limited subjective perspective. Seeing the situation from a different perspective, with the help of the consultant, may change the way the problem is perceived.

> An agency approached a child welfare consultant for help in establishing a program of interracial adoptions. The interest in such a program developed because the agency found itself with a growing number of minority children who were hard to place. In the discussion, the consultant raised the question as to whether or not the agency had considered establishing a program of service directed toward the black community in the area. As they continued to discuss this as a possible alternative the question for consultation was reformulated. It shifted from one concerned with consultant help in regard to establishing a program of interracial adoption to one of establishing a program in, and under control of, the local black community.

Since the primary function of the consultee is a clear exposition of the problem, it is not surprising that where consultation fails, consultants often attribute this to the "fact" that the consultee was not adequately prepared or that the purpose of the consultation was unclear. The consultee thus makes his principal contribution to effective consultation by "being clear in his own mind as to what his problem is and what he wants to discuss" (Robbins and Spencer, 1968, p. 364).

During the early expositional phase, the consultant makes some effort to determine the expectations of the consultee. If expectations are considerably at variance with what the consultant is ready and capable of offering, the consultant has the responsibility of helping the consultee redefine his expectations. Unless there is some mutual consensus as to how the participants in the interaction perceive the purpose, direction, and nature of the consultation and how they will proceed together to achieve these objectives, the consultation is not likely to be effective.

This is noted by Robbins, Spencer, and Frank (1970), who studied tape recordings of thirty-five consultations and had detailed interviews with consultees. Outcome measures were global statements of satisfaction-dissatisfaction in the experience, benefits derived from the consultation, and the extent to which suggestions made during the consultation were implemented by the consultees. An attempt was made to relate various components of the consultation event with the outcome measures. The analysis showed that there was a positive relationship between adequacy of consultant preparation, consultant interest in the consultation event, and global consultee satisfaction. Greater satisfaction was experienced when there was mutuality in perception of purpose on the part of consultant and consultee.

Consultees, like clients faced with a problem, have often sought informal consultation and have tried a variety of approaches before requesting formal consultation. Consequently, the consultant should, during this early expositional phase, ask questions about what has been tried, with what effect, in previously dealing with the problem. Nothing is likely to reduce confidence in the consultant so precipitously as to offer a solution which has already been tried without success. Exploring with the consultee the previous efforts he has made to solve the problem exemplifies the consultant's respect for the consultee and the readiness to credit him with what he knows and can do.

During this period, too, the consultant, like the supervisor, attempts an educational diagnosis. Is it that the consultee does not know what she needs to know in order to deal with her work problem effectively, or is it that she knows but cannot, for one reason or another, use the knowledge she already possesses, or is it that she knows, but doesn't know she knows? It not only is a question of what is the nature of the problem with which the consultee wants help but why she has such a problem.

Helping the consultee define her problem, helping her to define it in such a manner that it is linked with the kinds of expertise the consultant is capable of making available, and diagnosing the educational problem is part of the instrumental task achievement responsibilities of the consultant. In addition, throughout the entire interaction the consultant has the responsibility of helping the consultee feel psychologically comfortable—accepted, supported, and unthreatened. This is the relationship-expressive responsibilities of the consultant. But developing and maintaining a comfortable relationship helps achieve the tasks of consultation. The consultee may be unable to articulate her problem because she is not clear about what it actually is. However, she may be clear about the nature of the problem but hesitant to share it.

Consultation is a special instance of the more general category of interpersonal interactions between a person seeking help and a person offering help. Since this is the case, what we have learned about the facilitating conditions of helping situations generally is applicable to this particular type of helping situation. The consultant, if she is to be successful, has to be perceived as trustworthy, accepting, respectful, nonjudgmental, and ready and willing to permit the consultee to make his own decisions. The relationship is preferably voluntary, and as equalitarian and colleagual as possible. The interactional skills which the social worker, as social worker, has learned to implement in effectively offering service to agency clients are utilized to good advantage in the relationship with the consultee.

Each of these relationships is characterized by the same considerations. One must, in each of these relationships, start where the other person is; one must, in each of these relationships, individualize the other person; one must, in each of these relationships, engage the other person in actual participation in the interaction and demonstrate an empathic understanding of what he feels. One has to approach the other party in the relationship with tolerance, with flexibility, with compassion, and with a recognition that we are colleagues together in a difficult undertaking. While all of these considerations are applicable to the consultation relationship, none of this is unique to consultation. The effective consultee-consultant relationship and the effective worker client relationship are special examples of good human relationships. What makes for effective human relationships in one context is, as might be expected, similar to what makes for good human relationships in another context.

Explicitly articulating the need for help may be threatening and demeaning to the consultee, a confession of inadequacy which incurs the risk of rejection. An accepting, supportive relationship enables the consultee to share freely what needs to be shared if the consultant is to do his work effectively. Establishing and maintaining such a relationship is part of the expressive function of the consultant.

It is not surprising, therefore, that one study of school consultation which involved detailed interview with consultees found that personal characteristics associated with more or less effective consultants mirror much that has been said for some time in the literature on therapy generally. Thus positive qualities associated with effective consultants, as described by consultees, included such attributes as "warm," "friendly," "secure," "open," "sensitive," "competent," "accepting." Ineffective consultants were described as insecure, lacking in social skills, presenting a "professional façade," and offering "impractical recommendations."

The effective consultant, according to consultees, demonstrates

> the ability to understand and identify with the consultee's dilemma. Effective consultants appear to be particularly interested in the same problem as the consultee, or able to focus their interest on the consultee's concerns. The striking characteristic of very effective consultants that is not seen in other consultants is the ability to convey confidence in the consultee's ability to handle student problems, or to learn to do so, and the ability to reinforce teachers for trying to deal with these problems. In relation to this, these same consultants do not communicate any needs to control, subordinate, dominate, demean, criticize, or impose their own goals and values on the consultee. Likewise, they appeared able to influence their consultees and to accept influence from them without creating or experiencing feelings of defensiveness or resentment. (Behavior Science Corporation 1973, pp. 149–50)

The consultant-consultee relationship, as a professional transaction, is similar, once again, to the social worker-client relationship in that it is unilateral in the satisfactions it primarily offers. All professional relationships are designed to achieve the needs of one party in the relationship—in this instance, the needs of the consultee.

The consultation relationship is sometimes termed a coordinate relationship. This relates to the fact that mutual cooperation and contribution of effort on the part of all participants are necessary for the success of consultation. The consultant needs the input from the consultee in order to understand the problem and the problem situation. The consultee needs the consultant to help in identifying and sorting alternatives and in problem-solving. But this is not essentially different from the coordinate relationship needed in worker-client or supervisor-supervisee interaction.

And it is similar in another way. A feeling of trust, of security in the relationship not only results from the nature of the interaction the consultant is able to establish, it derives from confidence in the competence of the consultant. The consultee's trust in the consultant is heightened when he perceives that the consultant is capable of helping him. The transaction is one in which protective forces of the ego are contending with adaptive forces. Confidence in the consultant increases the adaptive rewards and strengthens the consultee's willingness to take risks because there is a likelihood of a problem-solving payoff.

REACTIVE PHASE
During the middle phase of the conference the task responsibilities rest primarily with the consultant. Having been informed of a clearly defined problem which is in his area of competence, the consultant at this point begins to react. There is a gradually increasing

> tendency to offer analyses in his attempts to interpret and clarify what the [consultee] has said and bring perspective to the problem. There is also a slow but steady rise in the consultant's tendency to offer opinions and evaluate statements. The consultant's tendency to give suggestions or recommendations also shows a gradual rise. (Robbins and Spencer, 1968, p. 367)

This reactive activity reaches a peak somewhere past the midpoint of the meeting. It is during this part of the conference that the consultant is actively at work helping the consultee to deal with the professional problem which she earlier articulated as the one with which she wanted help. Alternative solutions are presented for discussion; the worker is helped to understand the problem; intervention and problem management approaches are offered for consideration and their feasibility and acceptability discussed. The consultant helps the consultee "assess alternative means to alternative goals."

It is in this phase that the consultant earns his title. The consultant may be initially invested with a certain level of prestige. This derives from her position, her degrees, her professional affiliation and reputation. She must, however, earn the esteem which is a validation of her prestige. This depends to a considerable extent on how she actually performs in the consultant role. If she does poorly, if she appears not to "know her stuff," if she interacts without understanding and empathy, her prestige suffers as she fails to achieve esteem. Here, as in supervision, the consultant relates her expertise to the consultee in terms which are most relevant to the consultee's problems. She reacts not only to the needs of the consultee but to the person of the consultee. Her communication is addressed not only to what the consultee needs but to what the consultee can use. The specialized knowledge and expertise which the consultant brings have to be communicated in a way which is understandable, acceptable, and usable. Since it is the consultee who will act on and implement the outcome of consultation, it is important that he actually integrate it rather than passively accept it.

Here, as is true for all situations of interpersonal interaction, factors of personality intrude to determine the nature of interaction. As in supervision, a consultee's problems with authority may make him unduly critical, and predispose him to reject the recommendation of the consultant; a poor self-concept may result in a too ready, uncritical total acceptance of everything the consultant says. The consultant further needs to be aware that she is a party to the interaction and that her behavior, needs, and "hang-ups" condition the nature of the interaction.

Just as the consultant, while less active, is not passive during the preliminary exposition phase, similarly, during the reactive stage, the consultee, while less active, is not entirely passive. The consultee responds to the alternatives, suggestions, advice, and information being offered by the consultant. He makes efforts to understand what is being offered, to consider it carefully, to integrate it into his assessment of his work problem.

The line of decarmation between exposition and reaction is not fixed. Many of the questions asked by the consultant in helping the consultee with his exposition have interventive effects since they direct the attention and the thinking of the consultee along certain lines and shape his response. But while not clearly demarcated, it is true that there is greater emphasis on exposition at the early points in the contact and greater emphasis on interventive reaction at later points in the contact.

As in general social work practice, the consultant in interaction with the consultee acts as a catalyst, facilitator, motivator, role model; clarifies empirically determined optimum approaches to problems and clarifies consequences of different alternatives; helps the consultee to think more systematically and objectively about the problem he faces so as to increase his behavioral options; provides new knowledge not previously available to the consultee or frees-up old knowledge.

During this period the consultant asks pertinent questions not only to help the consultee better to understand the nature of the problem with which he wants help, but also in an effort to help focus the consultee's awareness on the most salient aspects of the consultation. The consultant's expertise lies in knowing just what are the most significant data required for problem solution.

The process of problem analysis in which the consultant engages the consultee is, in and of itself, helpful. It offers a model of an ordered, objective, systematic approach to solving this, and possibly similar, work-related problems.

We have previously noted that the expressive-facilitative relationship aspects of effective consultation are similar to those which social workers have regarded as required for effective work in other familiar contexts, i.e., in direct service to the client and in supervision.

The instrumental aspects of consultation, the procedures and techniques employed in implementing the purpose and objectives of consultation, are likewise similar to those employed by social workers in other contexts. The consultant's skill in performing such functions as "facilitating the expression and identification of problems, clarifying confused feelings, leading the consultee toward relevant and appropriate solutions and generalizing from specific situations" (MacLennan, Quinn, and Schroeder, 1971, p. 17) is essentially similar to the clinician's skill in performing such functions in contact with the client and those of the supervisor interacting with the supervisee.

In implementing these functions, the social work consultant employs the same skills employed in her clinical practice. For instance Bergan and Tombari (1975) did a detailed content analysis of 806 consultations tape-recorded by 11 psychologist consultants. They found that measures of consultant interviewing effectiveness were highly associated with both ability to identify the problem and with problem solution. They conclude that "when a consultant lacks interviewing skills, the consultant role itself is in jeopardy" (p. 224).

Since the primary professional task of the social worker qua social worker is to help effect change either in the client or in the client's social situation and since the worker has developed some procedures in performing this task in discharging his primary professional responsibilities, it is to be expected that these procedures would be carried over into the consultation person-change situation. In helping the consultee to solve his work-related problems, the consultant employs essentially the same change procedures he might employ in helping a client solve his life-related problems.

The knowledge of change procedures available in the casework and other clinical practice literature is of direct relevance to consultation. It is, therefore, not at all unexpected that some texts on consultation such as those by Fullmer and Bernard (1972) and Blake and Mouton (1976) are essentially texts on the process of planned change.

There is considerable disagreement on how people can be helped to change and considerable diversity in procedures thought to be most efficacious in achieving this objective. Consultants differ in their orientation to this question, and the consultant's theoretical presuppositions regarding the procedures which are most likely to effect change determine what consultants say they do in offering consultation (Woody, 1975). In the working-through process of helping the consultee solve her work-related problems, psychoanalytically oriented consultants and Rogerian-oriented consultants are likely to reflect, interpret, clarify, and support. The behavior modification-oriented worker will seek to identify behaviors which need to be changed, will be concerned with observing and recording levels of behavior emitted, with selecting change contingencies and applying such contingencies. The consultant concerned with changing organizational climate, decision-making, and communications patterns will more often be guided by the theoretical persuppositions deriving from Lewinian social psychology and the group interaction techniques developed by the National Training Laboratory (Reschly, 1976).

In discussing the consultants' activities in the working-through component of the consultation process, the social work consultation literature generally speaks of procedures deriving from psychoanalytic psychology and other nondirective approaches. This is because, until recently, these were the principal procedures applied in direct-service social work and mental health practice. It is anticipated that the social worker reader with direct-service practice experience is familiar with these procedures. Although behavior modification procedures have recently received increasing acceptance in the direct service sector, there are few instances of the application of such procedures to social work consultation (see, for instance, Fisher and Gochros, 1975, pp. 119–21). Behavior modification approaches to implementing the working-through aspects of consultation have received greater prominence in the literature of psychological consultation and counselor-guidance consultation (Mayer, 1972; Meyers, 1975; Morice, 1968; Randolph, 1972; Welch,

1973; Woody and Woody, 1971). The consultant may use behavioral modification procedures in attempting to change those behaviors of the consultee which negatively affect his performance effectiveness. More frequently, the consultee is helped by the consultant to become the "behavioral manager" of modification procedures targeted on the client. The consultant practices behavior modification through an intermediary change agent—the consultee.

A first-grade child was referred because of his lack of attention, cooperation, academic performance, and constant attention-seeking behavior. During the consultant-teacher conference, it was decided to designate "non-attentiveness" as the target-behavior. Nonattentiveness was operationally defined as turning around in seat, out of seat, handling objects irrelevant to the work task, pushing or hitting others, and talking at inappropriate times. Spot-checks were kept for five days (baseline), and showed the target-behavior to be occurring during 60 to 90 per cent of the spot-checks (mean 79 per cent). The modification program included moving the child to a different desk within the classroom (this being designated as his "working-seat"— his office) and ignoring his nonattentiveness. In addition, verbal praise was given upon the completion of each working assignment. A significant drop was registered in nonattentive behavior, from a mean of 79 per cent for baseline, to 33 per cent for the modification phase. A follow-up check at approximately three and one-half months, and again at four and one-half months showed the change to be lasting. The teacher reported significant gains in academic progress and peer relations from December through May (Morice, 1968, p. 258)

Some consultants who have experimented with helping consultee-teachers to develop a behavioral modification approach note the problems concerned with this (Abidin 1971, 1975; Hall 1971). Abidin (1975) details some of the objections to behavioral modification procedures and the difficulties which adhered to such programs of intervention occasionally for teachers. Teachers faced technical problems in remembering to reinforce on schedule, deciding whether behavior was on or off task, taking the time to give tokens if this was required. They were concerned about the effects on other children, the effects on the class interaction, and the effects on their teaching effectiveness of the focus required by the behavior modification program designed for one child. After detailed discussion with teachers Abidin, a behavior modification-oriented consultant, began to appreciate these considerations as "sincere reflections of problems which teachers were experiencing" (p. 52). He notes that these aversive factors may

> in part help to explain why the behavioral literature reports failure to generalize. Frequently teachers do not employ the technique they learned about one child in one sitting to another child in a different class—why in most school settings teachers frequently do not continue programs beyond two or three weeks unless a group of professors or graduate assistants are readily available to keep checking, prodding and reinforcing. (pp. 55–56)

In another article Abidin (1971) indicates that his experience suggests that

> in order for a teacher to work successfully in a behavior modification program she must have average and above average organizational ability; in fact being mildly compulsive is generally helpful. Teachers who tend to be non-directive, highly intuitive or very existentially oriented do not work out well in a behavior modification program. (p. 39)

Despite these considerations, behavioral modification is thought to be a particularly desirable consultation procedure because it can be taught with relative ease to professionals who carry the burden of direct application of a remedial program.

DIRECTIVITY IN WORKING THROUGH

The degree of directivity offered to consultants during the course of the consultation appears to be a dimension of considerable importance. We have touched on this earlier in discussing attitudes toward preparation for the consultation, pointing to the fact that some consultants deliberately choose not to prepare because preparation might suggest control of the consultation process by the consultant.

The Behavior Science Corporation in its study of mental health consultation to schools asked consultees to rate their consultants on their directivity and discussed this aspect of the consultant's functioning in personal interviews with the 265 consultees. They note that "while there is no quantitative data to support this, the impression of the research team is" that the group of more nondirective consultants "is most likely to be composed of the more recent consultants."

> Their characteristic style is to play down their role as an expert and an authority and to place considerable emphasis on the equalitarian relationship. In so doing, they deny their own resources to their consultees. They avoid providing any structure to the consultative relationship even to the point of withholding recommendations which are needed to facilitate the consultee's success. There is a feeling that unless advice is solicited, it represents a restriction of the consultee's freedom. It is efective only when requested. The irony here is that while the consultant is concerned about restricting the opportunity for the consultee to contribute his recources, the consultant actually is not sharing the responsibility of the relationship because he is wihholding his resources from the consultee. Consequently, little or nothing is derived from the relationship. Neither the consultant's resources—mental health knowledge and experience—nor the consultee's resources—experience and knowledge in the schools—are shared. The consultant withholds his influence because he doesn't want to restrict the consultee's opportunity for expression and growth. The consultee doesn't participate actively in the relationship because he doesn't understand what his role is.

Consultees didn't say that they don't know how to participate in an
equalitarian, collaborative relationship with someone they perceive
as an expert in an area where they are not. It was clear from the interviews, however, that many consultees are inexperienced in this
role and really don't understand that they play a vital part in this
relationship. They don't realize they are withholding their resources
because they aren't even aware of what their resources are. The
[more directive] consultants are ineffective for nearly the opposite
reasons. They commit the sins their non-directive counterparts are
so careful to avoid. They are insensitive to their consultee's needs,
imposing their own views and totally disregarding the consultee's
resources and the value of his participation in the relationship. (Behavior Science Corporation 1973, pp. 107–8)

As a consequence of these considerations the research concludes that the degree of directivity of the more effective consultants tends to be curvilinear—both too little and too much directivity appears to be undesirable. The more effective consultants
"are able to use the non-directive technique to advantage by
helping their consultees to take an active role in the consultation
process but at the same time they are not hesitant to assume active leadership when it was appropriate" (Behavior Science Corporation 1973, p. 109).

Comparing consultants rated [by consultees] as highly effective with
those rated as not very effective indicates that ineffective consultants
tend to gather at the two extremes of being either overly authoritarian or considerably non-directive. In contrast, more effective consultants appear to be highly flexible and adaptive to individual situations by being highly didactic (information giving) at times,
especially early in the initial consultation relationship, and gradually
becoming more non-directive as they have confidence in the consultee's ability to solve classroom management problems. (p. 66)

The researchers note that an inability to integrate the direc-
tive and nondirective approaches is frequently associated with
failure in consultation (p. 107).

INSTRUMENTAL AND EXPRESSIVE COMPONENTS

The balance between concern for interactional process and concern for problem-solving content such as advice and suggestions is another dimension pertinent to the consultant's activities at this working-through stage in the proceedings about which there is considerable controversy. A focus on concern with clinical process is most appropriate and applicable to both consultee-centered consultation and consultee-centered administrative consultation. It must be remembered, however, that studies cited above show these to be the least frequent types of consultation requested of social workers. Both client-centered consultation and program-centered administrative consultation require, for satisfaction of their objectives, some specialized expertise which makes available procedures, techniques, advice, suggestions—in short, the provision of definite, professional know-how in enabling the consultee to solve the problem he brings to consultation. These are problems brought by competent professionals who are not acting dysfunctionally, but lack the requisite knowledge to deal with the difficulties they face. Consequently, reflective responses, Socratic questions, a nondirective approach, clarification, and insight-oriented procedures are not altogether appropriate. This is not a clinical-equivalent situation, but more often one which requires communication of validated knowledge. Content, for the more frequently encountered types of consultation, is more important than process—which is not the same as saying that process is unimportant.

It is recognized that the social work consultation literature, echoing the mental health consultation literature, is heavily biased in favor of the greater importance of process. As Signell and Scott (1971) note, "it is consistent with emerging consultation philosophy that content itself is less important than process" (p. 298). It is felt that the most essential resource which the consultant brings is herself, lending herself "in a non-demanding, confident and trusting way to somebody struggling with a problem" (Beisser and Green 1972, p. 84).

The bias is functional. What mental health consultants have to offer primarily is largely skills in process interaction. This is not surprising, of course, since consultants have been, and are, first mental health practitioners. There is a comfort in continuity as well as a necessity in continuity. We can only do what we know and we feel most comfortable in doing that which we know. Consequently, mental health practitioners who become mental health consultants tend to practice mental health skills. The knowledge and skills which they have available are person-change skills. As Gilmore (1962) notes for the social worker-mental health clinician, "consultation is primarily an overlay on direct service methodology" (p. 9).

Such consultants obtain confirmation of the validity of their orientation from the fact that, dealing with mental health practitioners, some of the work-related problems brought to consultation are associated with personal difficulties of the practitioner—or are perceived as such by the consultant. A principal target for mental health consultation which, as noted above, receives recurrent attention in the literature is "theme interference"—a consultee-centered consultation problem which depends for its solution primarily on the process of interaction.

However, Moed and Muhich (1972) point to the possible inappropriate use of a process-oriented approach to consultation. Faced with a difficult problem "and not knowing a reasonable or feasible solution," the consultant might employ nondirective techniques. "An over emphasis on process at the expense of content can easily cover ignorance of the content under discussion while saving the face of the consultant" (p. 233).

Of further relevance is the report of a review of the "reaction of a group of Public Health Nurse consultees to their former consultants." The researchers note that the

techniques that the consultant employs to . . . achieve his goals represent an issue of some consequence. Workers in professional agencies are not patients and, in the main, do not wish to be treated

or manipulated by the consultant for any purpose. Frequently they
are aware of the consultant's attempts in this regard, however
subtle, and they respond in negative ways. (Eisdorfer and Batton,
1972, p. 172)

The more appropriate image is that of a technical expert
focusing his specialized knowledge and skill in helping the consultee solve a work-related problem. The knowledge and skill
brought to bear relate to the substantive content of the problem.
The focus is on problems; the aim is problem solution.

This emphasis on the specialized problem-solving expertise
of the consultant, either different from or beyond that which can
be made available by the supervisor, is congruent with the research on consultation outcome as perceived by consultees.
When consultees were asked to define a "good consultant" they
characterized him as one who gives "direct, concrete answers"
(Robbins and Spencer, 1968, p. 363). In another study the
achievements which most clearly differentiated "very successful"
consultations from "moderately successful" consultations, in the
view of the consultee, was the fact that "practical solutions to
problems were reached" (Mannino, 1972, p. 105). When asked
why they asked for consultation or what they hoped to achieve
from consultation, consultees most frequently listed obtaining
"help in solving a specific problem" (Robbins and Spencer, 1968,
p. 363), "help with formulation of treatment plans and goals," or
"help with disposition of case" (Mannino, 1970, p. 4).

The expectations of one group of consultees—teachers—as
perceived by consultants is outlined in a letter to educators from
a mental health center:

An educator usually calls on a consultant only after having made
considerable effort herself with a child. She is likely therefore to be
in a somewhat unraveled frame of mind and most anxious for action.
Moreover, other members of her school system may be looking over
her shoulder and implying that by now, for heaven's sake, she ought

to have gotten Johnny into line. Whereupon she finds herself in contact with a mental health specialist, frequently in possession of imposing titles, surely someone who will know what to do. And so the case is eagerly presented and an answer eagerly awaited.

There then follows a predictable little charade in which a good deal of discussion about what makes Johnny fail, shout, disobey, withdraw, etc., occurs. The consultant leaves, smiling with satisfaction, while the teacher fumes with rage because she still doesn't know what to *do* with Johnny. (Cooper and Hussal, 1970, p. 712)

As Brown (1967) notes:

It is not enough to "share common concerns," "communicate," and the like. It is necessary to *do* something about such concerns and communicate about an issue or its solution if one is to be an effective consultant. Sentiment and interaction are important constituents of human relationships but so is action and this should not be forgotten by the consultant. (p. 405)

The consultee frequently wants more than "help," he wants answers and solutions.

For example, twenty-one physicians participating in an evaluation study of consultation were "asked to check one or more qualities including academic knowledge, feeling of trust, personality or relationship as being most important to the consultation experience. Academic knowledge was perceived as most important," relationship with the consultant being perceived as of lesser importance (Vacher and Stratas, 1976, pp. 112–13). The researchers note that the focus on knowledge as the quality of prime importance suggests the perception of the consultant by the consultee as an expert. The consultees were further asked to "identify what elements from the consultation process were most helpful or brought about the most change in the way they worked with patients." While 72 percent of the responses were focused on help in dealing with patient problems ("dealing with difficult patients"; "different approaches to dealing with the mental patients"; "prescription of drugs for emotional illness"), only 10 percent of the responses checked "emotional support from the consultant which leads to feelings of increased self-confidence" as a significant "most helpful" element (Vacher and Stratas, 1976, pp. 114–15).

A study of the reaction of nonprofessional workers to consultation confirms these findings. The study concluded that

> consultants ranked the fact that they were liked and were considerate of the consultee as more important than the consultee did. . . . Consultation in communities is not just understanding communication and interaction! The consultant has been retained because there is a problem which needs action. It would appear that, while a personable relationship is pleasant, it is not as important to consultees as assistance in solving the problem which is the objective of consultation. (Neleigh *et al.*, 1971, p. 27)

Apparently, most consultees approach consultation with the commonly accepted definition which equates "consultant" with "expert." In response to this definitional structuring of the role they expect help and advice on specific matters. If the consultant fails to meet these expectations, the tendency is to regard the consultants as capable of providing the needed answers but unwilling to do so. Later the consultee might recognize the consultant's lack of omniscience and understand that the consultant's actions are the result not so much of unwillingness as inability. By that time, however, the discovery may no longer be of significance since the consultee has already written off the consultant as nonhelpful. As Réppucci *et al.* (1973) note in describing a failure in consultation to a correctional facility, "the belief that we *could* act effectively died later, but the sense that we *would* act effectively died very early" (p. 157).

The instrumental, problem-solving aspects of consultation are, according to the research, of principal importance to the consultees. Consultees were not indifferent to the relationship aspects. They did indicate preference for a consultant who communicated "sympathy," "friendliness," "interest," "receptivity," who was "personable, easy to get along with." However, they gave these considerations somewhat lower priority than the consultant's ability to help them solve their professional problems.

If you "know" you may not be able to communicate it, but unless you "know" there is nothing to communicate. A person may be an excellent teacher, may be a skillful master of the process of communication, have highly developed relationship skills, but unless he has the required knowledge, the results of his efforts are likely to be without any purpose. He is, as someone once said, a Good Humor man with an empty truck. The consultee, as a matter of fact, may prefer a bad humor man with a full truck of material that is useful for him in dealing with the problems that he brings. As Caplan (1970) says: "The success of consultation depends on the expertness of the consultant in regard to the content matter on which he is invited to help. A consultant who has excellent . . . communication skills will fail if the content of his message is poor because of lack of expert knowledge of the issue" (p. 224).

But, while stating this point of view with definiteness in order to balance what I regard as a faulty process-oriented bias in social work consultation, it is easy erroneously to move too far in the direction of the content-expert end of the dichotomy. The consultant needs to give some consideration to both the content aspects of the problem and the process components. To ignore one is as incorrect as ignoring the other. It is true that the prospective consultant, like the prospective supervisor, has to possess expertise. But if he possesses expertise only he is not yet a consultant. It is a necessary attribute but not a sufficient one.

In addition to his qualifications as an expert in some particular substantive area based on education and experience, the consultant also needs to possess the ability, and the desire, to share his expertise effectively. He needs to have some adequate interpersonal skills which enable him to establish an effective relationship. This provides the context which enables the consultant to communicate his stimulation, his knowledge, his suggestions or advice. Here, as in supervision, "to know" is not synonymous with teaching. It is this extra dimension which makes consultants out of experts.

Gilmore (1963) notes these general differences in orientation and comes to a similar conclusion:

> In a gross sense there seems to be a polarity in the objectives of social work consultation. On one side is the objective of enhancing the professional development of the consultee; on the other is the goal of helping to solve a consultee's specific work problem, be it case action or development of program policy. Thus consultants will vary according to the relative strength of their attention either to overall consultee understanding and functioning or to the specific problem solution in the situational context. Different consultants will emphasize either the educational-therapeutic or the problem solving components of consultation. However "one function does not preclude the other" and while there may be a difference in preference for one or another of these aims "essentially all social workers have a professional commitment to both." (p. 6)

A related aspect of these different orientations to consultation concerns the consultant's sensitivity to the kind of help the consultee needs in making effective use of consultation. Gouldner (1961) discusses this aspect of consultation as one of an "engineering" versus a "clinical" approach to consultation. The "engineer" accepts the client's statement of his problem at face value, offers validated solutions, and anticipates that the client will utilize the solutions to deal with his problem more effectively since he is rationally concerned with solving his problem. The "clinician," more perceptively, recognizes that the client's statement of his problem is only one of a number of elements he needs for an accurate understanding of the situation; that the "correctness" of the solutions he offers is only one of the factors which determine the client's reaction to the suggestions offered;

and that utility of the suggestions depends on many considerations other than the fact that they will help the client "solve"
his "problem." When the consultant

> recognizes that he has the problem of helping his client learn some-
> thing and when he recognizes that learning is not accomplished by
> fact-finding or communication techniques alone, then he is on his
> way to becoming a clinician. Unlike the engineer, the clinician seeks
> to identify the specific sources of the client's resistance to his finding
> and he attempts to develop and learn the skills enabling him to cope
> with resistance. (p. 651)

Tilles (1961) makes a similar point and illustrates it very
aptly in discussing business management consultations in which
consultants make a distinction between consultees seeking information and those asking for help. Asking for help involves acceptance, integration, and decision-making utilization of information.

Effective consultation requires something beyond a purely
cognitive, didactic, prescriptive statement of feasible solutions.
It requires some attention to the affective component in applying answers to problems.

Some judicious combination of both approaches is desirable. If industrial consultants are too heavily oriented toward
an "engineering" approach, focusing on solutions and neglecting
human relations, social work consultants tend to be too heavily
oriented toward a "clinical" approach, focusing on human relations and neglecting solutions, which derives from specialized
knowledge and expertise.

Social work consultants were asked by Kadushin and Buckman (1977) to identify their own orientation to social work consultation in terms of this dichotomy between content expertise
and process competence. A ten-point scale was offered, an-
chored at the extreme of the continuum by a statement presenting the opposing orientation. At one end of the scale consulta-

tion was defined as the "provision of technical assistance by an expert with specialized knowledge and identified skills in helping the consultee to solve work-related problems. The emphasis is on problem-solving; the task of the consultant is to share knowledge and experience with the consultee." The statement at the opposite end of the scale defined consultation "as an interpersonal process in which the relationship between consultant and consultee is employed to help the consultee develop his own solutions to work-related problems. The emphasis is on the therapeutic growth producing aspects of the interaction. The consultant's experience in a specialized area is less important than his human relations skills."

Placing these two distinctively different definitions of consultation at two ends of a continuum, we asked the respondent to select that point on a ten-point continuum which represented his own orientation toward consultation, with 1 on the scale representing the most extreme instrumental problem-solving orientation and 10 the most extreme expressive-process orientation. The mean response of 5.0 for the total group of consultants indicated an orientation which was almost an equal combination of expressive-process elements and instrument-technical assistance elements. The response was slightly weighted toward the instrumental-problem-solving orientation since the true midpoint was at 5.5 on the scale.

The school social workers as a group were more process-oriented than the total group of consultants, their mean score being 5.5 as against 5.0 for the total group. Child welfare-family service consultants were decidedly more problem-oriented, the group mean for such consultants being 3.3 on the scale. Psychiatric-mental health consultants, somewhat surprisingly, were less process- and more problem-oriented than the total group—the mean for these consultants being 4.2 as compared with 5.0 for the total group.

We further asked the consultants to check the continuum once again, but this time in terms of their perception of the orientation likely to be expressed by most of the consultees with whom they had worked.

The consultants viewed their consultees' orientation as being more heavily weighted toward the instrumental-technical assistance end of the continuum than their own. They saw their consultees as being clearly more task-oriented, interested in consultation for its value in problem-solving, and the consultant as a source of technical assistance in achieving this objective. With 1 representing the most extreme instrumental-problem-solving orientation and 10 the most extreme expressive-process orientation, consultees were rated 3.8 on the scale by consultants.

The mean scores for consultants and for their consultees as perceived by these consultants are noted on the following scales:

Scale 1
Consultants' Orientation
(N = 476)

| Consultation is the provision of technical assistance by an expert with specialized knowledge and identified skills in helping the consultee to solve work-related problems. The emphasis is on problem-solving, and the task of the consultant is to share his knowledge and experience with the consultee. | midpoint
↓
1 2 3 4 5 . 6 7 8 9 10
↑
mean | Consultation is an interpersonal process in which the relationship between consultant and consultee is employed to help the consultee develop his own solutions to work-related problems. The emphasis is on the therapeutic, growth-inducing aspects of the interaction. The consultant's expertise in a specialized area is less important than his human relations skills. |

Scale 2
Consultants' Perception of Consultees' Orientation
(N = 468)

midpoint
↓
1 2 3 . 4 5 . 6 7 8 9 10
↑
mean

Child welfare and family service agency consultees were perceived as more instrumental-problem-solving oriented than the total group of consultees, the mean scale rating for this group being 3.0 as against 3.8 for the total group. Psychiatric-mental health consultees and school social work consultees were perceived as only slightly less problem-oriented, the mean sale score being 3.2 and 3.3 respectively for these groups.

The questionnaire survey provided another unit of information which is relevant to this question. Having asked the respondent for a brief description of their most recent consultation experience, we then asked the consultants to explicate what, specifically, they did in helping the consultee. A list of possible alternative interventions was offered and the respondent was asked to check those employed in their last consultation experience. A total of 1,014 interventions was checked. Table 5 lists, in descending order, the percentage of this total for each intervention.

Table 5 Interventions Employed in Consultation: Percent of Total Nominations (N = 469)

Intervention	Percent
I provided information and/or acted as a resource person.	23.5
I helped the consultee identify and clarify the problem by asking appropriate questions.	20.8
I helped the consultee think of different alternatives to resolving the problems.	19.6
I listened carefully, made suggestions, and offered advice.	14.1
I provided an opportunity for the consultee to express his/her anxieties and frustrations.	10.5
I helped the consultees with a personal difficulty which was interfering with his/her ability to deal with the work-related problems.	3.6
I tried to educate and/or motivate the consultee toward the more effective use of consultation.	2.0
Other	4.7

Macarov (1968) asked about consultants' roles and activities in interviews with consultants and consultees associated with

social service programs for the chronically disabled and obtained
similar findings. Interviews were concerned with the interaction
in forty different consultations. Consultants felt that their most
important activity was giving advice and acting as an adviser was
their most important role. On the other hand, consultees tended
to see the principal role of the consultant as a resource person
and the most important activity as that of giving information (pp.
75–76). The consultant is seen as a "central data bank" making
readily available a variety of substantive and procedural information of value to the consultee in meeting his problems. While
consultees did rate providing factual information as the *most* important activity of the consultant as they perceived it, this was
very closely followed by the rating of giving advice as the second
most important activity (Table 57, p. 229). The role of "adviser"
in this study was defined as: "suggests course of action, indicates
preferred alternatives or outcomes, suggests ways of overcoming
problem"; that of "resource person" was defined as "gives information, refers to other sources of information, helps prepare
grant application, indicates sources of finances or personnel" (p.
164).

The picture which emerges is that of an actively involved
agent focusing on the problem brought by the worker, helping
to clarify the problem so as to understand clearly what is
needed, and then, through information, advice, suggestion, and
consideration of alternatives, seeking to assist in resolving the
problem. The consultant is less frequently concerned with the
use of the consultation in meeting the personal expressive needs
of the worker.

As might be expected, the kind of intervention offered is
related to the type of consultation requested. Those interventions most heavily dependent on relationship components in the
interactions ("provided opportunity to express anxieties, frustrations"; "helped consultee with personal difficulties") were more
frequently associated with requests categorized as "consultee-
centered consultation." Those interventions focused on task,

problem-solving responsibilities ("acting as resource person," "offering advice," "helping find alternatives") are more frequently associated with client-centered consultation and program-centered administrative consultation.

MAKING SOLUTIONS RELEVANT
In implementing his instrumental responsibilities in offering problem-solving information, advice, or suggestions,

> the consultant is limited by the fact that his specialized knowledge, more than likely, pertains to the class of problems rather than to the particular problem which is being experienced by the client. The consultant can cite general principles which hold in a majority of cases, but this is not likely to impress the client who wants to know what to do in his own immediate and unique situation. From the standpoint of the client the consultant's orientation is "too theoretical" in contrast to his own "practical" orientation. (Charters, 1956, p. 34)

The problem for the consultant, then, is to particularize the generalization, translating it into the specific situation.

We noted some of the advantages of the fact that the consultant comes from outside the agency. At this point, the disadvantages of the consultant's status as a stranger become apparent. The solutions which might be helpful in one context, in one agency, might be inapplicable or inappropriate in another agency. Agency rules, regulations, procedures, and traditions may rule out some solutions, however objectively helpful they might appear to be. The consultant needs to present advice, suggestions, alternatives with some awareness of the problem of feasibility and appropriateness. The consultant may suggest "good" solutions; only the consultee is in a position to suggest "workable" solutions—those which are within the normal operating procedures, established patterns, traditions, and regulations of the agency.

While it is true, as La Rochefoucauld says, that "we can give advice but we cannot give the wisdom to profit by it," the consultant has the obligation to give advice in a way which makes it optimally useful to the consultee. Like the supervisor who is also an indirect service worker, the consultant's "essential function is not to do but to enable others to do and the most brilliant ideas the consultant may have are useless until the consultee reconciles them and makes them his own" (Stringer, 1961, p. 89).

The consultant focuses relevant information so that it is appropriately applicable to the consultee's situation. The consultant has to provide help which is relevant to the consultee's frame of reference. The social work consultant to the teacher-consultee cannot expect that the teacher will become a social worker in the classroom; the psychiatrist-consultant to the social work consultee cannot expect that the social worker will become a "little psychiatrist" in his work with his client. The consultee has to maintain his own professional integrity and continue to perform in terms of his primary professional identification. What the consultant is being asked to do is to help the consultee extend his own professional skills "within his own mode of functioning." Consultation is more likely to be effective if the consultee can incorporate the suggestions into his repertoire of behaviors which implement his primary function: the teacher must be able to make the changes in behavior a part of his teaching procedure; the nurse, an aspect of nursing, and so forth.

The behavior required of an incumbent in implementing the role requirements of one profession may be quite different from the behavioral role requirements of another profession. A teacher acting adequately as therapist to a class may, as a consequence, fail to perform adequately as a teacher—the role for which she was hired and for which she is being paid. No great progress is made if, in gaining a therapist, we have lost a teacher or a nurse or an effective houseparent.

The suggestions which the consultant makes must not only

be technologically accurate and adequate, they must also be acceptable in terms of the value requirements of the social system in which the consultee operates. The consultee will tend to reject those suggestions which are not congruent with the value, mores, and procedural demands of the agency out of a desire to avoid conflict. But even if he were willing to risk conflict in attempting to implement such incongruent suggestions, he might not succeed. Working as a member of an organization generally requires the support and cooperation of others in the system for successful implementation of a plan. Not only the individual consultee but the organization itself must support desired behavioral change if it is to succeed.

We have noted above that freedom to accept or reject the consultant's recommendations clearly distinguishes consultation from supervision. However, the consultant having conviction in his recommendations may appropriately attempt to tip the scale of the consultee's ambivalence in their favor. The consequences for the ongoing consultation relationship may not be deleterious or disruptive. It may be helpful to call attention to the fact that in a study of factors relating to consultee satisfaction, Silverman (1974) found that feelings on the part of the consultee that he was obligated to accept the consultant's suggestions were positively related to an effective consultation relationship. Consultees "who feel obligated perceived a need for consultation and felt it to be useful. One of the definitions of obligation is an indebtedness to another for a service received. Some of the consultees may have expressed their gratitude for consultation with a sense of obligation" (p. 309).

While integration, incorporation, and utilization of the results of the consultation are clearly the task of the consultee, both the consultant and the supervisor have some responsibility for facilitating this.

Consultation as Support

In addition to offering problem-solving help, the consultant is frequently of value to the consultee at this stage in the process through providing emotional support of one kind or another. The consultant might sanction behavior about which the consultee might have some incipient anxiety and/or guilt. It is reassuring to a worker to have an expert approve or condone responses which the expert is recognized as being able to evaluate because of his special knowledge about the nature and effect of such responses. Working as a psychiatric consultant to nurses and nursery school teachers, Parker (1962, 1968) found that one of her most significant contributions lay in such sanctioning activity. In response to the myth of "the perfectly loving and understanding nursery school teacher" "there was evidence of guilt among the teachers for having feelings that, although perfectly normal and understandable, they felt they should *not* be having" (1962, p. 560). The consultant exculpated the teachers from feelings of guilt and anxiety when they were unable to love all the children, when they were not uniformly and consistently permissive, when they felt they understood a child's problem and yet were unable to solve it, when they were unable to help some children whose needs were obvious, when they felt dislike for a child and were unable to control its expression. Exculpation from a child psychiatrist consultant, for failures which lie in the consultant's area of expertise, is exculpation indeed.

Similarly, Zwick (1975), a social work consultant to schools, notes that "one of the crucial interventions early in consultative relationships is to assure teachers that limits are important to children and must be set to prevent anxiety" (p. 146) on the part of both teachers and pupils.

Consultation has a cathartic component which is supportive. The consultant provides an active, responsive, accepting listener with whom the consultee can discuss his work-related problems.

Given the opportunity of sharing some of the burdens of the job with such a listener tends, in and of itself, to be helpful.

Making consultation available has a supportive placebo effect.

> The very presence of the consultant or his availability by phone or visit when needed may be seen by the consultees as supportive. The consultant may often encourage the [consultee] to continue some of the same methods he is currently using in treating the [client] or he may inform him of a new method and reward him verbally when he uses a new type of treatment technique. (Vacher and Stratas, 1976, p. 53)

Support and encouragement from a supposed authority who comes from outside the agency may help to increase the worker's faith in himself, in his activities, and in the mission of the agency. The consultation provides stimulation and the opportunity for the worker to develop a special interest in some particular kind of work problem (Rosenthal and Sullivan, 1959, pp. 33, 34). It often reduces the guilt of the worker when he obtains confirmation from the consultant-expert that little real movement can be anticipated in some particular case. Even confirmation by the consultant of the consultee's diagnostic assessment of the problem situation is regarded as helpfully supportive (Lambert, Yandell, and Sandoval, 1975).

GROUP CONSULTATION
The group is frequently used as the context for consultation. A common format in consultation to social workers is, as has been noted, the group conference case presentation chaired by the psychiatric consultants.

Kadushin and Buckman (1977) found that 41 percent of the consultants offered group consultation either as the exclusive procedure or in addition to individual consultation.

In a national study of mental health consultation to schools, group consultation was found to be more common than individual consultation, individual consultation being more common in client-oriented consultation than in program-centered consultation (Behavior Science Corporation, 1973, p. 117; see also Caplan, 1972).

When consultation takes place in a group context, the consultant has to bring to the consultation a knowledge of group dynamics and some skill in facilitating effective group interaction. It is very easy to confuse group consultation with seminar teaching or group psychotherapy. In each instance a knowledge of group dynamics and process is consciously employed to achieve task purposes, and the principal vehicle is group discussion. The group has to be helped to focus on work problem-solving rather than engaging in what might amount to group therapy or personalized group counseling.

The advantages and disadvantages of group consultation are similar to those associated with group supervision (Kadushin 1976). Group consultation is a more efficient use of consultation time—it amplifies the impact of the consultant; it provides the potentiality for the emergence of a greater variety of possible solutions; peer pressure can be utilized as a vehicle for behavioral change. On the other hand, it presents difficulties in the coordination of consultee's schedules, it is an inappropriate context for dealing with highly individualized or possibly personalized problems, and for dealing with crisis situations. The group may inhibit some consultees. Its success depends on group composition, cohesiveness, and the consultant's competence in dealing with group interaction.

Consultation groups vary in composition. Some consist of members of a single profession. Less often, members of a number of different professions are involved as in a team. Sometimes the group consists of members all of whom are on the same hierarchical level—direct-service workers or administrators. Sometimes the levels are mixed, with direct-service work-

ers in the same group with supervisors and administrators (Rowitch 1968).

Termination

Having learned the problem, having drawn on his knowledge
and experience, on his specialized expertise, to offer some acceptable and feasible solutions or, alternatively, having helped
the consultee to find his own solutions, the task of the consultant
is substantially achieved. Participants move toward termination.
This appears to be a joint responsibility. It is concerned with
summing up, recapitulating, tying loose ends together, confirm-
ing that expectations have been met. In a sense, it looks back at
what has transpired during the conference. But it also looks
ahead. This stage of the conference is concerned with planning
the next conference, if one is to be scheduled, with determining
some procedures for follow-up, and with evaluating the results of
the conference.

Termination may involve some decision regarding the plan
for problem solution which includes the continued service of the
consultant in another role. With the agreement of the consultee,
she may welcome a collaboration in direct service to the client,
working along with the consultee to implement the plan. Or it
may be decided that the consultant should implement the plan
alone. The research consultant may be employed to do the research he discussed with the consultee; the in-service training
consultant may be employed to conduct the institute or workshop she planned with the consultee. The consultant should provide emotional support for the decision and the planning to
implement it. The consultant has to be sensitive to the effects of
his consultation feedback and take responsibility for helping,
both on an individual level and on an organizational level, with

some of the consequences of the advice and suggestions he offers. Setting in motion a change process "de-equilibrilizes" people and systems. Achieving a new equilibrium, which incorporates the consequences of the change the consultant is suggesting, may be part of consultation responsibility.

Inevitably, the consultant is a change agent. Her introduction into the agency system in interaction with its staff sets in motion a process which effects changes in individual practitioners and in agency operation. The purpose of such change is to increase the agency's effectiveness.

However, Seashore and Van Egmond (1961) make a distinction between consultants' responsibilities and change agent responsibilities. While all consultation implicitly involves the possibility of change, since a new element is being introduced into the system, change may not be a consciously deliberate aim of the consultant. Where such an objective is made explicit and is acceptable to both consultant and consultee, the consultant has definite change agent responsibilities. "As a consultant, aid can be given in the diagnosis of problems and the formulation of workable solutions. The [change agent] function involves helping members of the organization acquire the knowledge and skills necessary to implement changes and establish effective methods in reaching their goals" (p. 661).

While respecting the autonomy of the consultee, it is desirable for the consultant to indicate his continuing interest in the results of the consultation. This is supportive to the consultee who does not feel he is being summarily abandoned. The emphasis on autonomy and independence of the consultee implied in his responsibility for implementation may have negative effects, as Caplan (1970) points out: "The consultee may perceive the consultant as someone who wishes not to involve himself and get his own hands dirty in cases but only to operate in the privileged position of by-stander and critic—a sort of kibitzer in a chess game" (p. 123).

It is hoped that the conference will terminate with the consultee having a positive feeling toward the idea of consultation and what it has to offer. As a consequence of a negative experience the end of the consultation may mean the end of any further consultation.

Having terminated the contact with the consultee, the consultant is not yet finished with the consultation. There may be some contractual requirement to inform the worker's supervisor and/or the agency administrator about the contact. There may be some formal agreement for follow-up reports for which the consultant is obligated. There may be a requirement for, or the consultant's own desire to make, some record of the consultation, its purpose, the course it took, the outcomes that are likely.

Recording of the consultation is sometimes incorporated in the consultant's field reports or in the letters which follow between the consultant and the consultee and/or agency administration.

Respondents in the Kadushin-Buckman study (1977) were asked to list the ways "in which the consultation event became a matter of record." Thirty-three percent of the consultants indicated that following the consultation conference a "summary" was written up for the files by the consultant. An additional 5.5 percent noted that both consultant and consultee wrote a summary statement of the conference. In 23 percent of the cases, while a summary of each conference was not written up, there was ultimately a summary report written by the consultant when reviewing the contact. A disconcerting 21 percent of the responses indicated that "no formal provision of any kind is made for recording the consultation conferences." Only very rarely (2 percent) is the consultation session tape-recorded.

Such a response to record keeping is typical of consultants in the human services. A study of mental health consultation to schools concludes that "community mental health centers are definitely not prone to keeping records. In fact they appear to have a strong aversion to the task. Record keeping plainly is not seen as an important or necessary part of their job" (Behavior Science Corporation, 1973, p. 113).

There is yet another, final step to the process before the consultation events can be marked "terminated." The consultant has the responsibility of making some attempt at evaluation, to determine explicitly what went right, what went wrong, what was accomplished, what failed of accomplishment. This suggests some of the questions the consultant might ask himself in a retrospective evaluative review of the experience.

In addition to asking himself such questions for explicit consideration, the consultant should solicit feedback from the consultee. This seems to be rarely done. A study of mental health consultation to schools found that interviews with consultants showed that

> most report that they infer the state of affairs from what consultees tell them or the way that their consultees act but few actually confront their consultees directly with questions about how they feel about the program or things that they would like to change. The conclusion from these interviews has to be that in fact very little direct evaluation and feedback occurs between consultants and their consultees. . . . the primary method of evaluation and feedback is through an inferential process on the part of consultants. (Behavior Science Corporation, 1973, pp. 155–56).

> Only on rare occasions did we observe consultants asking for feedback from their consultees. Consultants are almost totally uninformed about their consultee's level of satisfaction. Because of the lack of feedback between consultants and consultees, consultants are simply not aware of the feelings of their consultees or of the impact of their services. This really appears to be more of an oversight on the part of the consultant than the result of planned neglect. (p. 114)

Termination should provide for some procedure for feedback not only to and from the consultee but also to agency or organization administration. This is desirable even though administration may no longer be directly involved in the ongoing consultation program. Continued support of the consultation program depends on administrative decision, and keeping administration informed of what is happening increases the probability of such support. Administration should be involved in the consultation program beyond the decision to grant permission for consultation.

Since the consultee also shares some responsibility for the nature of the interaction such retrospective evaluative analysis is incumbent on the consultee as well. However, since the consultant has primary responsibility for the conduct of the consultation, the requirement for such a formal or informal evaluation rests principally with him. If the consultant is going to continue to do consultation, such efforts at evaluation and any possible feedback he might be able to obtain are necessary for improvement of competence.

In addition to the informal self-evaluation engaged in by both consultant and consultee a more formal kind of retrospective evaluation-review might take place in a supervisory conference between the consultant and the consultant's agency supervisor. However, responses to a question regarding this in the Kadushin-Buckman (1977) survey indicate that this kind of evaluation review is likely to be infrequent. About 30 percent of the consultants indicate that no provision is made for supervision of consultation activity, and an additional 44 percent note that while there is no formal provision for such accountability, the consultant can arrange for such a conference with agency colleagues. In only 13 percent of the cases is provision made for regularly scheduled conference with an agency supervisor or administrator for review of consultation activities.

This speaks to the necessity for an informal and formal evaluation at the termination of each consultation in which the consultant is involved. There is a parallel responsibility for the field of consultation to evaluate the outcomes of evaluation through a formal program of empirical research. This activity will be discussed in the next chapter.

Summary

The chapter is concerned with the process of consultation following actual contact between consultant and consultee. The beginning, working-through, and termination phases of the process were discussed, some attention being given to the specific problem encountered in each of these phases in the process.

Chapter Six

Evaluation
and Problems

During the past decade all social programs and services have demonstrated some concern with evaluation in response to increasingly insistent demands toward accountability. Consultation services have been responsive to this demand, and there have been increasingly frequent attempts at researching the effects of consultation efforts. The most recent comprehensive review of the empirical studies concerned with the effects of consultation was done by Mannino and Shore (1975). They analyzed thirty-five consultation outcome studies conducted between 1958 and 1972.

The studies reviewed are concerned with changes in the consultee's attitudes and/or behavior which can be attributed to consultation, changes in the consultee's clients, and changes in the institution's structure or the system in which the consultee offers service. The largest number of studies are concerned with changes in the consultee, and the largest number of such studies available are concerned with teachers.

The studies tend to show that teachers changed significantly in their understanding of the child as a consequence of consultation, and they demonstrated a greater "psychological mindedness," greater leeway in accepting students' behavior and in dealing with individual differences, and greater sensitivity to emotional problems and their diversity. As a result of consultation, teachers "exhibited significantly greater interpersonal openness and acceptance of conflict" (p. 13). As a consequence, students tended to see those teachers who had received consultation as more "receptive," and the teachers seemed to "have a stronger, more assertive view of themselves and appeared to have achieved greater general comfort and self-satisfaction" (p. 14).

Nurses who received consultation, as compared with those who did not, also showed an improved understanding of their clients and a greater objectivity in responding to client problems.

In assessing changes in consultees' functioning with clients as a consequence of consultation, results are more equivocal. The research reviewers conclude that:

> Neither academic achievement nor behavior was changed in any consistent way as a result of consultation. Whether this is due to the problems inherent in conducting research on subjects who are not directly influenced by the experimental variable, to our lack of understanding of the linkage between the consultant, the consultee and the client or to actual difficulties in effecting change is unclear at the present time. (p. 11)

Only a very limited group of studies was concerned in any way with the organizational-system changes outcome of consultation, and here too the effects are doubtful.

A recapitulation of the findings of the thirty-five research projects was somewhat more optimistic. "In 69 per cent of the studies reviewed positive change was demonstrated on the consultee, client or system level or some combination of these" (p. 1). The nature of the research undertaken also showed a positive shift toward increasing sophistication of methodology employed. "More and more care is being given to an operational definition of consultation within a conceptual framework with increasing use of control groups and the testing of hypotheses" (p. 2).

Since 1972, the last year covered by the Mannino-Shore review, there have been a number of additonal studies of the effects of consultation. Once again most of these are with consultation to teachers. Tyler and Fine (1974) studied the effects of more or less intensive consultation by school psychologist to teachers:

> The findings were generally in favor of the intensive over the limited contacts between psychologist and teacher. In relation to the intensive experience teachers changed more in their understanding of the child and significantly in greater agreement with the school psychologist. Also the teachers indicated greater satisfaction with the intensive experience. (p. 15)

While a control group was employed, results obtained depended to a considerable extent on teacher's self-reports.

Mann (1973) also employed a questionnaire anonymously completed by teacher-consultees as the source of data for determining the effects of a program of consultation offered by psychology student consultants in a mental health consultation practicuum. Of twenty-five teachers who used consultation six said it made a difference in the behavior of children in their class, four said change resulted from a difference in their perception of the children, and twelve said that consultation had not made any difference (p. 185).

Ruckhaber (1975) reports on the effects of consultation conferences with elementary school teachers by a psychologist. Teachers were given "assistance in developing psychological insight into individual students and then, having these understandings translated into a series of recommendations that would, hopefully, result in the amelioration of the problem" (p. 64). The evaluation procedure consisted of reports from ten participating teachers, rating their response to the experience and the changes in students who were the subjects of consultation conferences. The teacher noted 45 percent of the students as having shown much improvement; 41 percent showed some improvement. Since there was no control group, attribution of such changes to consultation, if indeed they did actually occur, is an open question.

Brown and MacDougall (1973) used videotapes of teachers' classroom behavior in consulting with teachers about desirable changes in their performance. The focus of the study was on student change resulting from consultation with teachers, the specific hypothesis being that "given opportunities to examine, discuss and model behavior [in consultation] teachers will manifest behavior that results in increased positive self-perception on the parts of pupils in their classrooms" (p. 321). Sociometric procedures and self-perception forms were completed by students one week previous to the consultation and one week after the consultation program was ended. The data showed that students did "perceive themselves as more adequate in their relations with their classmates as well as their teachers" after the consultation experience. The pre- and post-test procedure implied that the students acted as their own controls in the experiments.

Meyer, Friedman, and Gaughan (1975) employed a more rigorous procedure in evaluating the effects of consultations. The consultants systematically recorded teacher behavior during one-hour observation periods over a series of days in order to establish a baseline regarding the frequency of "negative verbal interactions between the teacher and individual students, groups of students or the entire class" (p. 290). Following this a series of consultation conferences was held with the teacher at the end of which the classroom behavior was once again observed to determine the frequency of "negative" verbal interactions. Only three teachers were involved in the study, each becoming a subject at a different period in a stepwise fashion so that each acted as a control for the other. While the percentage of negative behavior for all three teachers decreased, for one of the three teachers such a reduction took place even before consultation was offered. The researchers cautiously conclude that the study "demonstrated a reduction in negative teacher behavior which may have been due to consultee-centered consultation for two teachers" (p. 293). This study is the first attempt to use direct systematic observation of consultees' performance in evaluating the effects of consultation.

Vacher and Stratas (1976) reported in an evaluation study that physicians receiving consultation "acquired more accepting attitudes toward others from observing the consultant's behavior" (p. 90). Physicians receiving consultation reported increases in job satisfaction and increases in confidence in working with psychiatric patients as compared with a control group of physicians who received no consultation (pp. 116, 118).

A project designed to evaluate the impact or effectiveness of mental health consultation services from twenty community mental health centers to twenty school districts used the response of consultees to consultation as the primary source of data (Plog, 1974). Information was obtained through interviews and self-administered questionnaires. Teacher-consultees felt they were more capable of dealing with a variety of mental health-related problems as a consequence of consultation. This was particularly true of behavior and emotional problems of students. A large percentage of teachers gave positive ratings to their consultation experience and indicated they would like to see the program continued.

Glaser (1977) reports on an evaluation of consultation provided to four different child care institutions. An "evaluator" visited the institution after each had received forty days of direct consultation. The "evaluator" assessed outcomes through inter-

views with institutional staff. No objective measures of change
were obtained. In the judgment of staff people interviewed, the
"general situation" at the institutions had improved as a consequence of consultation. Greater effectiveness of consultation was
associated with openness and flexibility on the part of the consultant, clear and unambiguous two-way communication between
consultant and consultee, and unequivocal support of consultation by the administration of the institution.

Social Work Consultation
Evaluation Studies

SOCIAL WORKERS AS CONSULTEES

One of the striking features of the evaluation consultation literature is the very limited number of studies involving social workers as consultees and the almost complete absence of control
studies of social work consultants identified as such. There are
three research studies which involve social workers as consultees.

Eisenberg (1958) studied the effects on clients of the use of
psychiatric consultation by social workers in a mental health
clinic whose "intake was restricted to welfare department foster
children" (p. 743). The psychiatrist consultants made a diagnostic evaluation of the child and, in consultation with the social
worker and supervisor responsible for the case, made recommendations as to treatment. After an interval varying from six to
eighteen months, the worker was asked to rate the client's adjustments, and the child was classified as either improved or
unimproved. A study of thirty-eight cases indicated that the
child was more likely to have shown improvement if the consultant's recommendations had been accepted and implemented by
the worker.

A study of the effectiveness of psychiatric consultation service to the staff of a vocational service agency which apparently

included social workers concluded that such "consultation did not appear to improve the effectiveness of the counselors' handling of their client's problems or to increase the professional development of the counselors in any recognizable aspects" (Ulmer and Kupferman, 1970, p. 326). The over-all conclusion was that psychiatric consultation did not fulfill the expectation of the agency in helping either staff or clients. Stephenson (1973) noted that a family and welfare agency serving a low-income population reduced referrals to an outside psychiatrist or psychiatric clinic as a consequence of consultation over a three-year period from 15 percent in 1968 to 3 percent in 1971. Reporting this bare statistic in the absence of any control, the reporter herself raises the question as to whether this results from increased "skills of the workers in handling clients with emotional disturbance" following consultation or if it is a reflection of the "growing painful disenchantment about the ability of the traditional psychiatric treatment programs to meet the needs" of a low-income group (p. 250).

Comparing the use of the local hospital emergency ward for children by the family and children's agencies as compared with similar agencies without consultation showed a less frequent use of such service by the agency workers who had consultation available. This "suggests" that "the consultation program led to increased ability of workers to cope with direct psychiatric disability, or perhaps workers felt more comfortable about handling disturbed youngsters knowing that psychiatric backup was readily available" (p. 257).

The researcher, noting the ambiguity about the effects of her efforts as psychiatric consultant to a social agency, concludes that "although subjectively this program has been a success and is described very positively by agency workers, its objective value is much harder to document" (p. 253).

Other kinds of outcomes of consultation have been reported descriptively rather than on the basis of research evaluation. For instance, as a result of consultation a social agency might feel more confident about serving a previously neglected group and widen its service intake. Kaphan and Litman (1966) describe such an outcome as a result of the consultation efforts of the Suicide Prevention Center in Los Angeles. The consultants offered help in evaluating the level of suicide risk of agency clients and offered supportive help, based on their expertise in regard to suicide, to allay the anxiety of the social agency workers.

> A worker called for consultation following a telephone application from a worker about a 14 year old boy who had taken six aspirin tablets. We were able to point out that in boys of this age who were not psychotic, a suicide attempt of this nature usually respresents "a cry for help" in a difficult family situation. When there is true assurance that the message has been received and that help is forthcoming this is usually sufficient in putting an end to the suicidal situation. It was agreed that the worker would offer an emergency interview to the family. (Kaphan and Litman, 1966, pp. 1359–60)

SOCIAL WORKERS AS CONSULTANTS

The limited evaluation material regarding social workers as consultants tends to be largely impressionistic and subjective. Confirmation of the value of consultation is presented in terms of clinical case histories or in testimonial reactions to consultation services offered.

Rosenthal and Sullivan (1959) report one experience of two psychiatric social worker consultants over a sixteen-month period with fourteen different social workers in a public child welfare agency. Because of staff turnover only a few of the workers in the project received consultation over the sixteen-month period. There were 164 consultation conferences on 56 individual cases. Evaluation of results was based on self-reports from consultees and their supervisors.

Workers and supervisors expressed satisfaction with the consultation conferences, and supervisors pointed to instances where they thought professional growth of the consultee could be attributed to consultation. It was felt, too, that most workers were more confident as a result of consultation. There was no explicit data available on the effects on clients of the consultation project. In general, evaluation results were subjective, indefinite, and lacking in specificity. The tentativeness of effects is noted in the over-all conclusion that "consultation made a contribution to strengthening and supporting supervision, to the professional development of the consultee and, at least in some instances, improved services to clients seems clear" (p. 36).

Nitzberg and Kahn (1962) attempted an evaluation of social work consultation services offered by a rural mental health clinic to welfare workers. They state that "while an accurate scientific evaluation of the effects of the program has not been carried out there is some evidence to indicate that it has been beneficial to the workers, their clients and hence to the community" (p. 92). However, the "evidence" offered is "evaluative comments elicited from the welfare workers," "remarks" from the social work consultants, and "impressions" of training program workshop leaders.

Rieman (1963) employed a focused interview with nurses who had been offered a social work group consultation program. Once again, although no statistics are offered, nor is there any indication as to how the interview material was analyzed, the author notes that consultation resulted in a greater understanding of human behavior, an increased recognition of the importance of relationship in professional activity, a better coordination of staff effort, and positive changes with reference to group process (p. 96).

Kitano (1961) studied the effects of a consultation on school administrations by a child guidance clinic team which included social workers. As a consequence of consultation, the administration's perception of the behavior of problem children shifted in a positive direction. The study does not conclude that the behavior of the children necessarily changed as a consequence of consultation but that the "opportunity for administrators to share anxieties, doubts, information—to communicate with the consultant in a crisis situation" (p. 133) resulted in changes in the administration's perception of the child's behavior.

Farley (1963) obtained evaluations of a program of social work consultation to public health nurses by soliciting feedback to the experience on an anonymous questionnaire. While no statistics are presented, comments indicated that respondents felt that as a result of consultation they had an increased understanding of patients' behavior, were better able to help their patients, and had a better concept of mental hygiene in general (p. 115). There were further comments that consultation resulted in a more accepting attitude by nurses toward their patients, and greater self-understanding.

Schmuck (1968) reported that teachers who had received consultation from social workers, among others, improved their approach to handling classroom problems and made changes in self-perception.

Macarov (1968) interviewed 39 consultees administering programs for the chronically disabled and obtained an evaluation of their consultation experiences with social work consultants. Taking the consultees' view at face value, 41 percent of the problems were solved and another 41 percent partially solved "following the consultation" (p. 54). Macarov notes first that these are subjective assessments and secondly it is not clear that whatever change was attained could unequivocally be attributed to the consultant's interventions. Consultees also reported "side gains" from the consultation experience in terms of personal growth, clarification of general work problems, helpful substantive and procedural information. It is interesting to note that 63 percent of the consultees felt that the problem encountered would have been solved in time without consultation (p. 55). The overwhelming majority of the consultees were positive in their attitude toward the consultation experience and indicated they would use such service again.

While social workers have made limited efforts to evaluate

their own consultation efforts, others have attempted to assess their consultation competence. Twenty-seven educators and thirty-one child care workers attending a conference on mentally retarded children responded to a questionnaire "which asked about their perceptions of the relative competence of four categories of professionals involved in assessing and treating childhood behavior disorders—social workers, pediatricians, psychiatrists and clinical psychologists" (Morrison and Thomas, 1975, p. 266). Assessment of competence was solicited with regard to specific interventions such as play therapy with children, counseling parents on managing child behavior, family therapy, and consultation with teachers. The resulting ranking for "consultation with teachers" indicated that social workers were perceived as less competent consultants than either psychiatrists or clinical psychologists but not significantly less competent than pediatricians (p. 267). The researchers note that "either the respondents were not aware of the competencies of a well trained psychiatric social worker or the term social worker too quickly conjured up the image of a harried and untrained caseworker whose working conditions made competence almost impossible" (p. 269).

There is little evidence in the evaluation material available that the broader social policy objective of consultation has been attained. There is no confirmation, for example, that as a consequence of a program of consultation the mental health climate of a particular community has been substantially improved, or that, as a consequence of consultation, there has been a measurable reduction in psychiatric casualties.

The primary preventive impact of consultation is still open to question. Since the greatest amount of consultation time and effort is devoted to client-centered consultation, the service can hardly be regarded as essentially preventive. Client-centered consultation is offered when the target of concern is already indicating impaired functioning and the consultation is primarily part of a treatment program.

A recent study of mental health center program operations

found "little interest in consultation as a means of primary prevention of mental illness" (quoted in Perlmutter and Silverman,
1973, p. 118). Such efforts were "undeveloped and undefined"
while their much greater effort was devoted to the more clearly
defined treatment functions of the centers.

One objective of consultation as an indirect service was to
extend the influence of professionally trained personnel, to
spread the consultant's know-how "through intermediation to a
large group of consultees, each of whom is in contact with many
clients" (Caplan, 1970, p. 21).

It is yet to be established empirically that as a consequence
of consultation social work expertise is amplified in this way, that
consultees make fewer or more selectively appropriate referrals
and more appropriate use of community resources, that agency
clients get better faster, that consultee-workers are more effective professionally, that agencies are more productive or that
they operate with better patterns of communication and decision-making and more job satisfaction. For the most part the effects of social work consultation or, for that matter, of consultation in the human services area generally, are still pretty much
an open question.

Problems in Consultation
Encountered by Consultants

One might discuss the problems of consultation on the level of
those faced by consultants in doing consultation. We have previously alluded to such problems in discussing some particular
aspects of consultation, such as, for instance, problems encountered by the consultants which are associated with entry into the
consultee agency. On the other hand, one might discuss problems of consultation faced by this kind of service generally. We
plan to do both. Starting with a presentation of some additional

problems generally encountered by consultants in doing consultation, we will then move on to present some of the problems currently facing consultation as an indirect service.

The Kadushin-Buckman survey listed problems that might be encountered by social work consultants and asked consultants to indicate the frequency with which such problems were in fact encountered. Twenty-one problems in offering consultation, derived from a review of the literature, were listed for respondent reaction. Nine were nominated by 40 percent or more of the respondents as being encountered "frequently" or "ocasionally." Table 6 lists these problems and the percentage of respon-

Table 6 Problems in Offering Consultation Encountered by Consultants, Frequency in Percentages

(N = 479)

Problem in Offering Consultation	Frequency Encountered	
	Frequently	Occasionally
I am aware of problem situation which might be helped by consultation, but the prospective consultee or his agency is not interested in accepting consultation.	17.1	51.4
The consultee has done little to prepare for the consultation and does not use the consultation effectively.	9.9	57.9
Agency policy gets in the way of effective consultation.	13.7	51.2
Not enough time is provided for consultation.	20.4	41.2
There is a big discrepancy between the expectations of the consultee and what I can offer.	8.2	46.0
The job of a consultant is difficult because the most difficult situations are referred to me for help.	16.5	38.4
I find that I have been given insufficient and/or irrelevant information to do a good job of consultation.	4.6	44.7
The agency administration is not fully committed to the idea of consultation, and I consequently do not receive the sanction and support I need to work effectively.	11.8	36.1
Since few non-social work consultees have any clear idea of what social workers know and can do, this presents a problem for me as a social work consultant.	10.0	35.0

dents encountering them "frequently" or "occasionally." The problems are listed in descending order of frequency when both responses are combined.

The identified problems *least* frequently nominated as a cause of concern for the consultants included: (1) being accepted as a consultant because of sex difference between consultant and consultee; (2) anxiety occasioned by the fact that the consultee was more familiar with the agency and its procedures than was the consultant; and (3) anxiety resulting from working as a guest in a host agency without the support of the consultant's own agency structure and the presence of own agency colleagues.

The problems identified most frequently suggest considerable ambivalence on the part of agency, administration, and consultee regarding consultation. They indicate perception by the consultant of resistance to consultation, lack of commitment in terms of agency policy, planning and available time, and limited consultee investment in preparation for consultation. This may reflect lack of confidence in the effectiveness of social work consultation and/or the low priority given consultation in a conflict between the effort required for productive consultation and competing job demands.

The following additional problems received a modest level of nomination as either being encountered frequently or occasionally by the consultants:

1. "If the agency has no clearly defined policy regarding use of consultation, both I and the consultee are apt to be confused about procedures."

2. "I am not sure I can be of help in a particular situation for which consultation has been requested. I do not have the required expertise."

3. "Even if the consultant believes that the consultee has the right to reject her/his advice and suggestion, the feelings generated by such rejection present a problem for me when it happens."

4. "Being accepted as some kind of expert makes it difficult for me to resist the temptation to believe I know all the answers."

5. "Consultees identified with professions that have greater prestige than social work are reluctant to accept social work consultation from me."

6. "In working with professionals other than social workers (doctors, nurses, etc.) there is a problem in learning the professional language of the consultee."

7. "In working with professionals other than social workers it is difficult for me not to try to make them into quasi social workers."

8. "The consultee is resistive to consultation because he fears being 'therapized' or caseworked."

Problems Relating to Consultation as a Service

DEFINITION

There is a problem which derives from the difficulty in formulating a clear-cut definition of consultation. In exemplification of this abiguity Robbins and Spencer (1968) say that "consultation is an interpersonal process that is in many ways like teaching, has some elements in common with supervision and occasionally looks like psychotherapy" (p. 362).

Reviewing the literature of consultation research in 1971, Mannino notes that "efforts have been made to differentiate [consultation] from other kinds of activities which use the helping relationship as its base such as counseling, supervision, collaboration and in-service training." He concludes, however, that thus far, judging from the research literature, these efforts do not appear to be too successful. As a result, it is "exceedingly difficult to speak of consultation in a manner which conveys to the reader a clearly recognizable activity" (p. 2). Erikson's statement in 1966, when she attempted one of the earliest studies of social work consultation, appears to reflect substantially the current situation. She noted then that there was "no generally ac-

cepted definition of consultation, no common terminology
among its practitioners—activities subsumed under consultation
were varied and ideas about the nature of consultation were not
always clear" (pp. 284–85).

We noted above that consultation was among the services
which mental health centers were obligated to offer under the
Community Mental Health Construction Act of 1963. Subsequent study of the program operations, however, indicates
that "consultation appeared to be the least understood of the essential services [offered by the mental health centers] both in
terms of what it is supposed to consist of and what it is supposed
to accomplish" (Perlmutter and Silverman, 1973, p. 117). As a
partial consequence of the amorphous definition of consultation,
a limited percentage of mental health center time (5.5 percent)
is devoted to consultation. Of the five principal mandated services offered by federally funded mental health centers, only
emergency services were allocated less time. Rather than ex-
panding, consultation time showed a decline between 1972 and
1973 (Bass, 1974, p. 2).

If there is a difficulty in clearly distinguishing consultation
from other forms of indirect service, there is an even more difficult problem of definition in clearly differentiating social work
consultation from the consultation efforts of other, related professionals. The social work consultant to the public schools is not
easily distinguishable from the psychology consultant or the
guidance and counseling consultant. The activities of the social
work consultant and the psychologically minded nursing consultant in a geriatric facility are often indistinguishable. The activities of the social worker offering consultation as a staff member
of a mental health center are not clearly differentiated from his
clinical psychology staff colleagues who are performing similar
functions.

For many social workers offering a consultation function,
the activity may be an integral part of their other, more primary
job responsibilities. The consultation function is not clearly and

explicitly defined as such. As a consequence, the consultation function has low visibility and is often neither consciously identified nor analyzed and, therefore, not clearly defined.

However, it would appear that the problem of differentiating social work consultation from other forms of human services consultation is a reflection of a more pervasive problem, one that faces the profession as a whole. This is the problem of defining the special unique expertise of social work. It is one manifestation of the problem of explicating the "functional specificity" and "exclusive competence" which differentiate social work from related disciplines.

Cabot, a physician who championed the employment of medical social workers as consultant members of a hospital service team, was forced to raise the question as early as 1909. He noted: "The value of the social worker and his proper recognition are considerably limited by the fact that he cannot recognize himself or tell you what the value of his profession is. He is an expert. *But in what is he an expert,* what is his field of knowledge or skill?" (Cabot, 1909, p. 38).

The problem of defining the special expertise of social workers becomes particularly acute in offering consultation service since the consultant is identified by the nature of the expertise he purports to represent. The listing of situations in which social workers acted as consultant, reported in chapter 3, tends to indicate a great diversity of concerns, projecting a picture of diffuse competence. It is difficult to identify a clear core of common expertise unique to social work, emerging from the statements of situations for which the social workers were offering consultation. There is a reiterated concern with the social aspects of the problem for which social work consultation help was being solicited and a recognition of the social worker expert's knowledge of social service resources. Social workers were recognized as having a special knowledge of social work, but the nature of the special knowledge was vaguely defined.

Some of the social work consultants were offering consultation as a consequence of having developed expertise over a period of time in performing a specialized job function. A social worker might be a Medicaid regulations specialist, or a group home specialist, or an intercountry adoptions specialist. The expertise reflected special job experience rather than a uniquely specialized body of professionally based knowledge shared with other social work professionals, all of whom had completed a common educational program. The consultant's expertise tended to be idiosyncratic rather than representative and characteristic of expertise expected of most social workers. Here a problem of definition faced by the profession generally makes for a problem in differentiating and defining the nature of social work consultation in particular.

This is a problem both for the consultant and the consultee. The consultant has to feel secure in a unique competence which he has defined for himself with the aid of the profession and which is recognized and accepted by others as reflecting his professional affiliation. The consultee has to be able to select from the pool of human service professionals that person whose professional label connotes the particular kind of expertise he needs for helping him to solve his difficulties. The image of the profession's unique, differentiated, specialized expertise needs to be relatively strong and clear if the consultee is to perform his task of selection and the consultant his task of helping in line with consultee's expectations.

It also presents a problem for continuing support of social work consultation efforts. Unless there is clarity about the contribution which social workers qua social workers (rather than as idiosyncratic experts) can make and a validation of such contribution, there is less likelihood that social policy will include mandated support for such efforts. The experience of social work consultation to nursing homes is illustrative of such a problem.

CONSULTATION LEVEL AND OBJECTIVES
Another problem faced by consultation as a service, which reflects an analogous controversy in the profession generally, re-

lates to the objectives of consultation. There are a number of different ways in which this problem is stated. Should the emphasis of consultation be primarily preventive or should one accept the more modest, more limited remediation objectives of consultation? Should consultation be directed primarily toward systems change or should consultation be directed primarily toward indirect service to particular clients in difficulty? Should the consultant be social change-oriented or clinically oriented? The problem is sometimes expressed in terms of defining the nature of the problem. Does the consultant define the client's problem as one to which the client makes a significant contribution, or is the problem primarily the consequence of the social system's dysfunctions, the client being primarily an unfortunate victim of circumstances beyond his control?

The controversy is sometimes couched in terms which contrast a medical model approach to problematic situations as against a systems approach. The medical model presupposes that the problem is centered in the client, that the professional's responsibility is to attempt a diagnosis of the problem and then offer the prescriptive interventions that will resolve the problem. There is the further question as to whether the prescriptive interventions are directed toward developing insight, greater awareness and self-understanding, as is true for the psychodynamic, nondirective interventions, or toward unlearning and relearning, as is true for the behavioral modification procedures. But whatever the choice of corrective procedure, the consultee's client is the focus of such change efforts, the goal being the more effective mobilization and utilization of the client's own resources for more effective social functioning.

The systems orientation takes a wider view, seeing the client as embedded in a complex context, the ecosystem, with which the client interacts. The problem results from difficulties in the interrelated network which includes the worker and the organization he represents as well as family and neighborhood community. The focus of change efforts is more widely distributed, with more deliberate concern for effecting changes in the

institutional context as well as in the consultee's-client's relationship with, and response to, the context. The broader social
change-systems orientation points to a kind of advocacy consultation.

Costin (1975) expresses the social action point of view when
she points to the consultant's responsibility to "alleviate stress on
groups" of clients by bringing about changes in the system of the
institution-client relations (p. 135).

Another consultant representing a mental health facility
takes this position as well. Stechler (1974) notes that the

> ultimate goal is to change the philosophical stance of the agency that
> you are dealing with. There are many people who say that a consul-
> tant should never get himself into that position. I don't believe that.
> I think you have to be very careful about how you go about it. If
> you say I am the kind of person who helps people with their stated
> needs, that's fine, that is a stance that we should all take as clini-
> cians, and I think for us to have social goals for our individual pa-
> tients is a very dangerous, very questionable practice. But for us to
> have social goals for institutions within our society, I think, is not a
> questionable practice. Let me get more concrete and specific about
> this. If we think, for instance, that certain kinds of philosophical and
> organization changes within the Boston school system would be bet-
> ter for the mental health of children in that area, I think it is our job
> to start to move into an advocacy position with the Boston school
> system and try to get them to change their ways so that they be-
> come partners with us in serving the mental health of children. (p.
> 87)

Schild, Scott, and Zimmerman (1976) express a different
orientation. In offering a program of social work team consultation to schools they note "that the team's approach was not to alter
the educational goals, format, or structure of the school but
rather to work within them. The team wished to help the
teachers increase their understanding of the children's problems
within their own conceptual framework." (p. 493). They approv-

ingly quote one of the requirements listed by Hallowitz and Van Dyke (1973) for effective teamwork with the school to the effect that the consultant "must understand and accept the teacher's frustrations and negative feelings toward a child whose behavior has gone beyond the limits of the school's situation and has thwarted their primary education function. A dangerous pitfall can be the clinician's overidentification with the child and his defending the child against the school" (p. 393). Here the orientation is toward the contribution which the client rather than the system makes to the difficulties encountered.

The consultant's entitlement to act as a systems change agent is questioned by Beisser and Green (1972). They write that the consultant "must *respect* the organizational and disciplinary goals of the consultee organization and *respect* their competence to carry them out. If he does not he is likely to become a saboteur attempting to 'right' the errors of the agency or to act as a 'change agent' which would be inappropriate to his function" (p. 26).

In support of the more limited, more restricted role for social work consultants, one might argue that even if it is agreed that the system makes a significant contribution to the problems the client faces, do social workers have sufficient expertise to advocate particular kinds of reforms in complicated system arrangements? If educators themselves, who are far more knowledgeable and sophisticated about the educational structure and programming, are still undecided about the value of such changes, for instance, as the open classroom, on the basis of what research, knowlege, and special experience can social workers advocate such changes? In each instance in which social work consultants work for change in systems arrangements it is their responsibility to provide the hard evidence which would support the need for recommended changes. They would further need to make some assessment of the consequences of such recommended changes on other aspects of the system's operations. This requires a detailed knowledge of the total system's operation rather than only the social services sector. These are the kinds of responsibilities which face a conscientious consultant in deciding on an orientation to the task he is given.

Here, once again, the controversy regarding the desirable primary orientation of the social work consultant between being clinically oriented as against systems-oriented, between being primarily concerned with symptom change or systems change, reflects a still undecided debate within the profession generally as to the principal focus of professional efforts.

THEORY vs. PRACTICE

In consultation, as in supervision, the ideological strain toward an equalitarian peer relationship, suggested by the theory of such relationships, is contradicted by the realities of status difference between participants in the relationship. While, in general, both consultee and consultant are equally competent in their own chosen field of specialization, while, in general, each is deserving of respect for what he knows and can do, for the purpose of the consultation they are clearly not equal. It is, in fact, the very inequality in their knowledge, skill, and expertise that brings them together and provides the *raison d'être* for the encounter. The consultant vis-à-vis the consultee, like the supervisor vis-à-vis the supervisee, may be "first among equals"— but he is clearly first.

One empirical study of the consultation interaction suggests that the consultant's attempt to redefine an inherently "unequal" situation as an "equalitarian peer" relationship is confusing and runs counter to consultee expectations. The researchers conclude by noting that "the status relationship most desirable to facilitate" the consultation "is that of an authoritative expert rather than that of an equalitarian peer." By retaining "a position of authority based on their expert knowledge . . . less confusion would develop between the expectations of the consultee and the behavior considered appropriate for the consultants" (McClung and Studen, 1972, p. 42).

A study of mental health consultation to schools notes that, "the attempt of the consultant to create an equalitarian relationship results in feelings of anxiety and frustration in the consultee which may be expressed as resistance or lack of trust or confidence" (Behavior Science Corporation, 1973, p. 49).

Theoretically desirable procedures are not often followed in practice. For instance, it is theoretically clear that consultees should be informed about, and actively participate in, consultation planning efforts. However, one empirical study which covered the consultation practice of eighteen mental health agencies using data obtained from eighty-six consultants and ninety-two consultees concluded that

> in the majority of programs observed, the consultees actually receiving service are not aware of the origins of the consulting relationship nor are they privy to the consulting contract. The consultees' lack of knowledge about their consulting contract explains the ambiguity and confusion reported by them regarding their expectations about consultation. (McClung and Stunden, p. 36)

In general, it is said that, "the actual behavior of professionals doing consultation is not congruent with the theoretical principles [of consultation] which they report as directing their efforts . . . the position taken by most consultants toward consultation is highly idiosyncratic and dependent upon the consultant's traditional professional background" (McClung and Stunden, p. 39) and familiar frame of reference. This may reflect the lack of specific training in consultation available to many consultants, which is an additional problem.

TRAINING

We noted in chapter 1 that relatively few graduate schools of social work offer an adequate program of training in consultation. This is reflected in the lack of special preparation for consultation with which most social worker consultants undertake this task. Kadushin and Buckman (1977) asked their respondents to indicate the extent of their formal training in social work consultation. Table 7 summarizes the response.

Table 7 Training Experience of Social Work Consultants in Percent
(N = 466)

Training Experience	Percent
I have never had any formal training in consultation.	35.0
I have completed a course in consultation given by a school of social work.	21.7
I have completed a short institute or workshop given by a school of social work.	12.7
I have completed a short in-service institute or workshop given by the agency.	11.8
I have attended special one or two-day meetings on consultation at a national or regional social work conference.	10.7
Other (please specify)	8.2
Total	100.0

The responses suggest that many social work consultants have had no formal training and that, for many others such training has been of rather limited duration. As a consequence, beginning social work consultants are often made anxious by the fact that they assume responsibilities for consultation with some uncertainty as to what is involved and how to go about it.

It is often presumed that given the professional training of social workers they would have little difficulty in translating such skills to the demands of consultation. Further formal training in consultation is regarded as unnecessary or redundant. While much of what the social worker knows as a professional can be readily adapted to consultation and while much can be acquired on the basis of experience in consultation, formal training in the process of consultation per se appears to be helpful.

Thus "exemplary" consultation programs to schools, as noted by consultees, were more likely to have consultants who had received some formal training in consultation as compared with consultants in programs noted as "average" or "nonex-emplary" (Behavior Science Corporation, 1973, pp. 104, 145).

Few consultants have any considerable experience in the role of consultee. Consequently, anticipatory socialization to the new role through participation in a variety of consultation events is not available as a training procedure for many consultants.

The problem of preparation is further compounded by vir-tue of the fact that, having accepted consultation responsibilities with little if any special training, most consultants are not pro-vided with adequate supervision. In response to a question regarding the supervision available to consultants 30 percent in-dicated, as noted above, that the agency made "no provisions for supervision of my consultation activities." Only 13 percent "meet regularly with agency supervisor or agency administrator" for a review of their work.

The national study of mental health consultation to schools found this lack of supervisory assistance to beginning consultants characteristic of community mental health center program operation. The study concludes that,

> considering the orientation of the community mental health centers which allow each consultant to do his own thing and to work in-dependently, the new consultant really is provided with very little training or assistance from other individuals on the community men-tal health center staff who have more experience within the school as consultants. (Behavior Science Corporation, 1973, p. 112)

FUNDING SUPPORT FOR CONSULTATION

Nagging questions about what human services consultation is and what it can do, make such programs vulnerable to attenua-tion of continuing support. Consultee organizations have ap-parently not been sufficiently impressed with what such pro-grams can offer to indicate a willingness to fund such programs.

The problem of the precarious nature of continued support for consultation programs was cited by Plog and Ross (1973) in

reporting on their experience in the national study of mental
health consultation to schools. On going into the field to study
the operation directly they

> were shocked to discover that many of the centers report the com-
> mon difficulty that they literally cannot give their services away.
> Consultation is most often provided without charge to school dis-
> tricts but, even then, there aren't many takers. Of the twenty
> centers visited, we estimate that only four or five [consultation ser-
> vices] stand a chance of surviving on the basis of community support
> if and when supporting funds from the [federal government] are
> withdrawn. (p. 66).

For the most part, human services consultation programs
are currently not self-supporting but operate largely on the basis
of funding contributed by the federal government and, to a more
limited extent, on the basis of fees from consultee organizations.
Continuation of such programs without support funding is ques-
tionable. For instance,

> in August, 1974 the General Accounting Office reported to the
> House SubCommittee on Public Health and Environment, that
> without continued federal assistance a number of existing [com-
> munity mental health center] services, especially outpatient care for
> low income groups and consultation and education for all would
> probably be curtailed or eliminated at many Centers. (Foley, 1976,
> p. 131)

It is true, of course, that part of the funding problem faced
by consultation services results from the fact that no third-party
payments are available for reimbursement of consultation efforts.
Consultation competes with other auxiliary services of possible utility to consultee agencies and organizations for the increasingly scarce funds available for purchasing such assistance.
Thus mental health consultation to the school competes with
remedial reading and remedial mathematics programs, special

education programs for the handicapped, enrichment programs for the culturally disadvantaged, and so forth. Consultation has to validate clearly its claims to being of competitively greater value to the consultee system, in this instance the schools, if priority in budget allocation is to be given to such a service.

Summary

Research evaluating the effects of consultation was reviewed. While there is some evidence to indicate that client-centered and consultee-centered consultation has the desired impact, there is little evidence to substantiate the effects of the broader objective of consultation. There is very limited research available evaluating the effects on social work consultee performance or on the effects of social work consultation.

Problems encountered by consultants in performance of their role were reviewed as well as some of the significant problems faced by consultation as a service.

References

Abidin, Richard R. 1975. "Negative Effects of Behavioral Consultation." *Journal of School Psychology* 13: 51–56.
—— 1971. "What's Wrong with Behavior Modification?" *Journal of School Psychology* 9: 38–42.
Aikin, Dorothy. 1957. "Psychiatric Consultation in the Family Agency." Unpublished Ph.D. dissertation, University of Chicago.
—— 1965. "Psychiatric Consultation in Social Agencies." *Canada's Mental Health* 13: 45–50.
Albini, Joseph. 1968. "The Role of the Social Worker in an Experimental Community Mental Health Clinic: Experiences and Future Implications." *Community Mental Health Journal* 4: 111–19.
Alderson, J. 1971. "The Challenge for Change in School Social Work." *Social Casework* 52: 3–10.
Alt, Edith S. 1959. "Social Work Consultation in Prepayment Medical Care Plan." *American Journal of Public Health* 49: 350–54.
Altrocchi, John. 1972. "Mental Health Consultation." In Stuart E. Golann and Carl Eisdorfer, eds., *Handbook of Community Mental Health,* pp. 407–508. New York, Appleton-Century-Crofts.

——, Carl Eisdorfer, and Robert F. Young. 1968. "Principles of Community Health in a Rural Setting: the Halifax County Program." *Community Mental Health Journal* 4: 211–20.

Altrocchi, John, C. Spielberger, and Carl Eisdorfer. 1965. "Mental Health Consultation with Groups." *Community Mental Health Journal* 1: 127–34.

Anderson, Claire H., and Thomas Carlsen. 1972. "The Midway Project on Organization and Use of Public Assistance Personnel." In Robert L. Barker and Thomas L. Briggs, eds., *Undergraduate Social Work Education*—a Report, pp. 17–28. Washington, D.C., Government Printing Office.

Anderson, Luleen S. 1976. "The Mental Health Center's Role in School Consultation: Toward a New Model." *Community Mental Health Journal* 12: 83–88.

Argyris, Chris. 1961. "Explorations in Consulting-Client Relationships." *Human Organization* 11: 121–33.

Arnold, Mildred. 1941. "The Specialized Child Welfare Consultant." In *Proceedings of the National Conference of Social Work, 1941.* New York, Columbia University Press.

Austin, Michael S., and Jordan I. Kosberg. 1976. "Social Work Consultation to Nursing Homes." Unpublished; mimeo. 14 pp.

Babcock, Charlotte. 1949. "Some Observations in Consultative Experience." *Social Service Review* 23: 347–57.

Bartlett, Harriett M. 1942. "Consultation Regarding the Medical Social Program in a Hospital." In *Consultation.* Menasha, Wis., George Banta Publishing Co.

Bass, Raylyn D. 1974. *Consultation and Education Services—Federally Funded Community Mental Health Centers, 1973.* Washington, D.C., National Institute of Mental Health; Division of Biometry, Survey and Reports Branch.

Baxter, Edith. 1956. "Administrative Supervision vs. Consultation." *Child Welfare* 35: 19–24.

Beck, Ruth. 1945. "The Child Welfare Consultants in a State Department of Public Instruction." *The Family* 25: 387–91.

Beckhard, R. 1966. "An Organization Improvement Program in a Decentralized Organization." *Journal of Applied Behavioral Sciences* 2: 3–25.

Behavior Science Corporation. 1973. *Evaluation of the Impact of Com-*

munity Mental Health Consultation Services on School Systems: Vol. II. *The Dynamics of School Consultation.* Washington, D.C., National Technical Information Service, U.S. Department of Commerce.

Beisser, Arnold, and Rose Green. 1972. *Mental Health Consultation and Education.* Palo Alto, Calif., National Press Book.

Bell, Cynthia. 1975. "Legal Consultation for Child Welfare Worker." *Public Welfare* 33: 33–40.

—— 1976. "Medical Consultants: Appropriate Selection and Utilization in Child Welfare." *Child Welfare* 55: 445–58.

Bellak, Alan. 1975. "Behavioral Consultation in Community Mental Health Centers." *Behavior Therapy* 6: 388–91.

Berg, Robert. 1959. "The Casework Consultant in Camp." *Journal of Jewish Communal Services* 35: 405–13.

Bergan, John R., and Martin L. Tombari. 1975. "The Analysis of Verbal Interactions Occurring during Consultation." *Journal of School Psychology* 13: 209–26.

—— 1976. "Consultation Skill, Efficincy in the Implementation and Outcome of Consultation." *Journal of Psychology* 14: 3–14.

Bergen, Bernard J., Robert J. Weiss, Charlotte J. Sanborn, and Charles Solow. 1970. "Experts and Clients: the Problem of Structural Strain in Psychiatric Consultations." *Diseases of the Nervous System* 31: 346–402.

Berkowitz, Morton I. 1975. *A Primer on School Mental Health Consultation.* Springfield, Ill., Charles C. Thomas.

Berlin, Irving N. 1964. "Learning Mental Health Consultation: History and Problems." *Mental Hygiene* 48: 257–66.

—— 1969. "Mental Health Consideration for School Social Workers: a Conceptual Model." *Community Mental Health Journal* 5: 280–88.

—— 1974. "Some Lessons Learned in 25 Years of Mental Health Consultation to Schools." In *The Workshop of Mental Health Consultation,* pp. 18–48. Washington, D.C., National Technical Information Service, U.S. Department of Commerce.

Bernard, Viola. 1954. "Psychiatric Consultation in the Social Agency." *Child Welfare* 33: 3–8.

Bettleheim, Bruno. 1958. "Psychiatric Consultation in Residential Treatment: the Director's View." *American Journal of Orthopsychiatry* 28: 256–65.

Bindman, Arthur. 1959. "Mental Health Consultation Theory and Practice." *Journal of Consulting Psychology* 23: 473–82.

Blake, Robert R., and Jane S. Mouton. 1976. *Consultation*. Reading, Mass., Addison-Wesley Publishing Co.

Blanton, Smiley. 1925. "The Function of the Mental Hygiene Clinic in the Schools and Colleges." In Jane Addams *et al., The Child, the Clinic and the Parents*. New York, New Republic.

Boehm, Werner. 1956. "The Professional Relationship between Consultant and Consultee." *American Journal of Orthopsychiatry* 26: 241–48.

Bonkowski, R. J. 1968. "Mental Health Consultation and Operation Head Start." *American Psychologist* 23: 169–73.

Bourn, C. S. 1973. "Planned Change in a Welfare Organization." *Human Relations* 26: 113–26.

Brockbank, R. 1968. "Aspects of Mental Health Consultation." *Archives of General Psychiatry* 18: 267–75.

Brody, Celia. 1951. "Psychiatric Consultation in a Family Counseling Agency." *Jewish Social Science Quarterly* 28: 151–57.

Brown, Jeanette A., and Self Ann MacDougall. 1973. "Teacher Consultation for Improved Feelings of Self Adequacy in Children." *Psychology in the School* 10: 320–26.

Brown, S. 1966. "Psychiatric Consultation for Project Head Start." *Community Mental Health Journal* 2: 301–6.

Brown, S. W. 1967. "Pragmatic Notes on Community Consultation with Agencies." *Community Mental Health Journal* 3: 399–405.

Bush, E. D., and C. E. Llewellyn. 1958. "A Statewide Experiment with Psychiatric Consultation." *Public Welfare* 16: 127–30.

Cabot, R. C. 1909. *Social Services and the Art of Healing*. New York, Moffat, Yard and Co.

Caplan, Gerald. 1959. *Concepts of Mental Health Consultation*. Washington, D.C., United States Government Printing Office.

—— 1970. *The Theory and Practice of Mental Health Consultation*. New York, Basic Books, 1970.

Caplan, Ruth. 1972. *Helping the Helpers to Help*. New York, Seabury Press.

Carter, Bryan D. 1975. "School Mental Health Consultation: a Clinical Social Work Interventive Technique." *Clinical Social Work Journal* 3: 201–10.

Charters, W. W. 1956. "Stresses in Consultation." In *Supervision and Consultation*, Pamphlet, p. 7. Washington, D.C., Adult Education Association.

Cherniss, Cary. 1976. "Presenting Issues in Consultation." *American Journal of Community Psychology* 4: 13–24.

Chesler, M. A., and Fred Arnstein. 1970. "The School Consultant: Change Agent or Defender of the Status Quo?" *Integrated Education* 8: 19–25.

Child Welfare League of America. 1975. *Standards for Foster Family Service Revised*. New York, Child Welfare League of America.

—— and Peat, Marwick and Mitchell Co. 1976. *Child Welfare in 25 States—an Overview*. Washington, D.C., Peat, Marwick and Mitchell Co.

Cohen, Louis D. 1964. *Consultation: a Community Mental Health Method. Reports of a Survey of Practices in Sixteen Southern States*. Bethesda, Md., Southern Regional Education Board and National Institute of Mental Health.

Cohen, Mariette B., Gail Abma, and Phyllis Selterman. 1972. "A Position Paper on Psychiatric Consultation in a Public Welfare Agency." *Public Welfare* 30: 11–15.

Coleman, Jules. 1947. "Psychiatric Consultation in Casework Agencies." *American Journal of Orthopsychiatry* 27: 533–39.

—— 1953. "Contribution of the Psychiatrist to the Social Worker and Client." *Mental Hygiene* 37: 249–58.

Collins, Alice H., and Diane N. Pancoast. 1976. *Natural Helping Network—a Strategy for Prevention*. Washington, D.C., National Association of Social Workers.

Cook, Maxwell A. 1970. "Ten Commandments of Consultation." *Public Welfare* 28: 303–5.

Cooper, Saul, and Leonard Hassol. 1970. "Mental Health Consultation in a Preventative Context." In H. Grunebaum, ed., *The Practice of Community Mental Health*, pp. 703–33. New York, Little, Brown and Co.

Core, H. M., and D. R. Lima. 1972. "Mental Health Services to Juvenile Courts—Consultation and Education for Court Personnel." *Hospital Community Psychiatry* 23: 174–78.

Costin, Lela. 1975. "School Social Work Practice—a new Model." *Social Work* 20: 135–39.

Council on Social Work Education. 1962. *Official Statement of Curriculum Policy for the Master's Degree Program in Graduate Professional Schools of Social Work.* New York, the Council. Documents No. 61-91-15R4.

Cowen, Emory L, Mary A. Trost, and Louis D. Izzo. 1973. "Nonprofessional Human-Service Personnel in Consulting Roles." *Community Mental Health Journal* 9: 335–41.

Daggett, D. R., *et al.* 1974. "Mental Health Consultation Improves Care of Aged in Community Facilities." *Hospital and Community Psychiatry* 25: 170–73.

David, G. 1967. "Building Cooperation and Trust." In A. J. Marrow, D. G. Bowers, and S. E. Seashore, eds., *Management by Participation,* pp. 95–109. New York, Harper & Row.

Davis, Alice T. 1956. "Consultation: a Function in Public Welfare Administration." *Social Casework* 37: 113–19.

Davis, W. E. 1957. "Psychiatric Consultation—the Agency Viewpoints." *Child Welfare* 36: 4–9.

Decker, James H. and Frank H. Itzin. 1956. "An Experience in Consultation in Public Assistance." *Social Casework,* 327–34.

Dinkmeyer, Don, and Jon Carlson. 1973. *Consulting: Facilitating Human Potential and Change Processes.* Columbus, Ohio, Charles E. Merrill.

——, eds. 1975. *Consultation: a Book of Readings.* New York, John Wiley and Sons.

Drake, R. 1946. "The Use of Consultants in a State Agency." *Public Welfare* 4: 88–90.

Dworken, Anita L., and Edward P. Dworken. 1975. "A Conceptual Overview of Selected Consultation Models." *American Journal of Community Psychology* 3: 151–59.

Eisdorfer, Carl, and Lois Batton. 1972. "The Mental Health Consultant as Seen by His Consultees." *Community Mental Health Journal* 8: 171–77.

Eisenberg, Leon. 1958. "An Evaluation of Psychiatric Consultation Service for a Public Agency." *American Journal of Public Health* 48: 742–49.

Erickson, Mildred H. 1966. "Consultation Practice in Community Mental Health Services." Unpublished D.S.W. thesis, University of Southern California.

Evans, D. A. 1973. "Problems and Challenges for the Mental Health Professional Consulting to Community Action Organization." *Community Mental Health Journal* 9: 46–52.

Family Service Association of America. 1953. *Practice in the Use of Perceived Psychiatric Consultation in 17 Private Family Service Associations of America Member Agencies.* New York, the Association.

—— 1956. *Psychiatric Consultation in the Family Service Agency.* New York, the Association.

—— 1969. *Family Service Statistics.* New York, the Association.

—— 1975. *Family Service Statistics—Facts and Trends on FSAA Member Agencies 1975.* New York, the Association.

Fanshel, David. 1976. "Status Differential: Men and Women in Social Work." *Social Work* 21: 448–54.

Farley, Bernice C. 1963. "Individual Mental Health Consultation with Public Health Nurses." In Lydia Rapoport, ed., *Consultation in Social Work Practice,* pp. 99–116. New York, National Association of Social Workers.

Feldman, Frances L. 1969. *Consultation: a Social Work Tool for Knowing More, Doing Better and Engaging Others.* San Diego, NASW Southwest Regional Institute; mimeo.

Fisher, Joel, and Harvey L. Gochros. 1975. *Planned Behavioral Change: Behavior Modification in Social Work.* New York, Free Press.

Fogelson, Franklin. 1970. "How Social Workers Perceive Lawyers." *Social Casework* 51: 95–101.

Foley, Henry A. 1975. *Community Mental Health Legislation.* Lexington, Mass., Lexington Books.

Forstenzer, H. M. 1961. "Consultation and Mental Health Programs." *American Journal of Public Health* 51: 1280–85.

Frankel, Fred H.., and Eleanor Clark. 1969. "Mental Health Consultation and Education in Nursing Homes." *Journal of the American Geriatrics Scoiety* 17: 360–65.

French, Lois M. 1940. *Psychiatric Social Work.* Cambridge, Mass., Harvard University Press.

Fuchs, Jerome H. 1975. *Management Consultants in Action.* New York, Hawthorne Books.

Fullmer, D. W., and H. W. Bernard. 1972. *The School Counselor-Consultant.* Boston, Houghton Mifflin Co.

Galleissich, J. 1973. "Organizational Factors Influencing Consultation in Schools." *Journal of School Psychology* 11: 57–65.

Garrett, Annette. 1956. "Psychiatric Consultation." *American Journal of Orthopsychiatry* 26: 234–40.

Gaupp, Peter G. 1966. "Authority Influence and Control in Consultation." *Community Mental Health Journal* 2: 205–10.

Gebbie, M. Kristine. 1970. "Consultation Contracts: Their Development and Evaluation." *American Journal of Public Health* 60: 1916–20.

Gilbert, Ruth. 1960. "Functions of the Consultants." *Teachers College Record* 61: 177–87.

Gilmore, Mary H. 1962. "The Consultative Role with Personnel Involved in Licensing Child Welfare Services." Indianapolis, Third Great Lakes Regional Licensing Workshop; mimeo, 9 pp.

—— 1963. "Consultation as a Social Work Activity." In Lydia Rapaport, ed., *Consultation in Social Work Practice*, pp. 33–50. New York, National Association of Social Workers.

Glaser, Edward M. 1977. "Consultation in Institutions for Child Development." *Journal of Applied Behavioral Science* 13: 89–109.

Glasscote, Raymond M., and Jon E. Gudeman. 1969. *The Staff of the Mental Health Center*. Washington, D.C., Joint Information Service, American Psychiatric Association and the National Association for Mental Health.

Glidewell, John C. 1959. "The Entry Problem in Consultation." *Journal of Social Issues* 15: 51–59.

Goldman, George. 1940. "The Psychiatrist and the Function of the Private Agency." *American Journal of Orthopsychiatry* 10: 548–66.

Goldmeir, John. 1971. "Applying a General Systems Approach to Consultation in Public Welfare." *Public Welfare* 29: 310–19.

Golembiewski, R. T., and A. Blumberg. 1967. "Confrontation as a Training Design in Complex Organizations." *Journal of Applied Behavioral Sciences* 3: 525–47.

Gorman, Joanna F. 1963. "Some Characteristics of Consultation." In Lydia Rapoport, ed., *Consultation in Social Work Practice*, pp. 21–31. New York, National Association of Social Workers.

Gouldner, Alvin. 1961. "Engineering and Clinical Approaches to Consulting." In Kenneth Warren *et al.*, eds., *The Planning of Change*, pp. 643–52. New York, Holt, Rinehart, and Winston.

Green, Rose. 1965. "The Consultation Process." *Child Welfare*, 425–30.

—— and Maurice Hamovitch. 1962. "Education of Social Workers for Mental Health Consultation." *American Journal of Orthopsychiatry* 32: 225–26.

Green, S. L. 1956. "The Use of the Consultant." *American Journal of Orthopsychiatry* 26: 234–52.

Griffith, Charles R., and Lester M. Libo. 1968. *Mental Health Consultants—Agents of Community Change*. San Francisco, Jossey-Bass.

Grossman, Frances K., and Donald Quinlan. 1972. "Mental Health Consultation to Community Settings: a Case Study of Failure to Achieve Goals." In Stuart E. Golan and Carl Eisdorfer, eds., *Handbook of Community Mental Health*, pp. 617–40. New York, Appleton-Century-Crofts.

Group for the Advancement of Psychiatry Reports. 1975. *The Psychiatrist and the Public Welfare Agencies*. New York, Mental Health Materials Center.

Guttman, Daniel, and Barry Willner. 1975. *The Shadow Government*. New York, Pantheon Books.

Halfoene, John, and Frances Welch. 1973. "Teacher Consultation Model: an Operant Approach." *Psychology in the Schools* 10: 494–97.

Hall, R. V. 1971. "Training Teachers in Classroom Use of Contingency Management." *Educational Technology* 11: 33–38.

Hallowitz, David, and Catherine Van Dyke. 1973. "The Role of the School as Part of the Treatment Program." *Child Welfare* 52: 392–99.

Haylett, Clarice H. 1969. "Evolution of Indirect Service." In H. R. Lamb, D. Heath, and J. J. Downing, eds., *Handbook of Community Mental Health Practice*, pp. 289–304.

—— and Lydia Rapoport. 1964. "Mental Health Consultation." In Leopold Bellak, ed., *Handbook in Community Psychiatry*, pp. 319–39. New York, Grune and Stratton.

Hetznecker, William, and Marc Forman. 1974. *On Behalf of Chidren*. New York, Grune and Stratton.

Hitchcock, J., and W. E. Mooney. 1969. "Mental Health Consultation." *Archives of General Psychiatry* 21, 353–58.

Horn, Eugene, *et al.* 1969. "School Mental Health Services Offered without Invitation." *Mental Hygiene* 53: 620–24.

Insley, Virginia. 1959. "Social Work Consultation in Public Health" and "Program Consultation." In Gerald Caplan, ed., *Concepts of Mental Health and Consultation*, pp. 215–46. Washington, D.C., U.S. Printing Office.

Iscoe, Iva, *et al.* 1967. "Some Strategies in Mental Health Consultation." In Emory L. Cowen, Melvin Zax, and Elmer A. Gardner, eds., *Emergent Approach in Mental Health Problems*, pp. 307–30. New York, Appleton-Century-Crofts.

Jacobson, S. R. 1953. "The Psychiatric Social Worker as Visiting Case Consultant to Community Social Agencies." *Journal of Psychiatric Social Work* 22: 98–104.

Jarvis, P. E., and S. E. Nelson. 1967. "Familiarization: a Vital Step in Mental Health Consultation." *Community Mental Health Journal* 3: 343–48.

Joint Commission on Mental Health and Illness. 1961. *Action for Mental Health*. New York, Basic Books.

Kadushin, Alfred. 1976. *Supervision in Social Work*. New York, Columbia University Press.

—— and Myles Buckman. 1977. "National Survey of Social Work Consultants." *Social Work* (in press, 1978).

Kane, Raymond. 1966. "Social Work Consultation to the Priest." *Catholic Charities Review* 50: 4–10.

Kaphan, Marvin N., and R. E. Litman. 1966. "Suicide Consultation: a Psychiatric Service to Social Agencies." *American Journal of Psychiatry* 122: 1357–61.

Karno, Marvin, and Donald A. Schwartz. 1976. *Community Mental Health—Reflection and Explorations*. New York, Spectrum Publications.

Kaufman, Irving L. 1956. "The Role of the Psychiatric Consultant— Workshop: the Use of the Consultant." *American Journal of Orthopsychiatry* 26: 223–33.

Kazanjian, Vard. 1972. "A Study of the Elements of Process as They Are Revealed in Mental Health Consultation." Unpublished Ph.D. dissertation, California School of Professional Psychology, San Francisco.

——, Sherry Stein, and William Weinberg. 1962. *An Introduction to*

Mental Health Consultation. Washington, D.C., Public Health Monograph No. 69.

Keith-Lucas, Alan. 1954. "Some Necessary Skills in Child Welfare Consultant Relationship." *Public Welfare* 12: 100–102.

Kiester, Dorothy S. 1969. *Consultation in Day Care.* Chapel Hill, University of North Carolina, Institute of Government.

Kindelsperger, Walter L. 1958. "Differentiating the Role of Child Welfare Consultant from the Role of Public Assistance Casework Supervisor." Unpublished Ph.D. thesis, School of Social Service Administration, University of Chicago.

Kitano, Harry. 1961. "Perceptual Changes in School Administrators Following Consultation about Problem Children." *Journal of Counseling Psychology* 8: 129–34.

Koch, William. 1967. "A Stance Toward Helping." *Adult Leadership* (December), 202–4, 236–39.

Lambert, Nadine, Wilson Yandell, and Jonathan H. Sandoval. 1975. "Preparing School-based Psychologists for School Based Consultation." *Journal of School Psychology* 13: 68–75.

Leader, Arthur. 1957. "Social Work Consultation to Psychiatry." *Social Casework* 38: 22–38.

Levine, Murray, and Adeline Levine. 1970. *A Social History of Helping Services.* New York, Appleton-Century-Crofts.

Levinson, A. I., and R. C. Reff. 1970. "Community Mental Health Center Staffing Patterns." *Community Mental Health Journal* 6: 118–25.

Levinson, Frances T., and M. Robert Gombert. 1951. "The Social Agency and the Psychiatrist." *Jewish Social Service Quarterly* 28: 143–50.

Liben, F. 1969. "Psychiatric Consultaton for a Local Welfare Center." *American Journal of Public Health* 59: 2013–21.

Lifshutz, Joseph, T. B. Stewart, and A. M. Harrison. 1958. "Psychiatric Consultation in the Public Assistance Agency." *Social Casework* 39: 3–9.

Lipowski, Z. J. 1976. "Psychiatric Liaison: Past, Present and Future." In Robert O. Pasnau, ed., *Consultation-Liaison Psychiatry,* pp. 1–28. New York, Grune and Stratton.

Lippitt, Ronald. 1959. "Dimension of the Consultant's Job." *Journal of Social Issues* 15: 5–12.

—— 1975. "Consulting Process in Action." *Training and Development Journal* 29: 38–41.

—— and Gordon Lippitt. 1975. "Consulting Process in Action." *Training and Development Journal* 29: 48–54.

Loeb, Martin. 1968. "Concerns and Methods of Mental Health Consultation." *Hospital and Community Psychiatry* (April) 111–13.

Lounsberry, John W., and Diana Q. Hall. 1976. "Supervision and Consultation Conflicts in the Day Care Licensing Role." *Social Service Review* 50: 515–23.

Macarov, David. 1968. *A Study of the Consultation Process—the Report of an Evaluation Committee.* New York: New York State Communities Aid Society.

—— *et al.* 1967. "Consultants and Consultees—the View from Within." *Social Science Review* 43: 283–97.

MacLennan, Beryce W. 1974. "Strategies of Community Mental Health Program Consultation." In *The Workshop of Mental Health Consultation.* Washington, D.C., National Technical Information Service, U.S. Department of Commerce.

—— 1975. "Program Development and Gaining Access in Community Mental Health Consultation to the Schools." In Fortune V. Mannino, Beryce W. MacLennan, and Milton F. Shore, eds., *The Practice of Mental Health Consultation,* pp. 61–75. Adelphi, Md., National Institute of Mental Health.

——, Robert D. Quinn, and Dorothy Schroeder. 1971. *The Scope of Community Mental Health Consultation and Education,* Public Health Service Publication 2169. Rockville, Md., National Institute of Mental Health.

—— 1975. "The Scope of Mental Health Consultation." In Fortune V. Mannino, Beryce W. MacLennan, and Milton F. Shore, eds., *The Practice of Mental Health Consultation,* pp. 3–24. Adelphi, Md., National Institute of Mental Health.

McClung, Franklin B., and Alastair A. Stunden. 1970. Consultation to Programs for Children. Rockville, Md., National Institute of Mental Health; revised.

Maddux, James F. 1950. "Psychiatric Consultation in a Public Welfare Agency." *American Journal of Orthopsychiatry* 20: 754–64.

Magner, George W. 1970. "Social Work Practice in Mental Health, 1955–1969." *Abstracts for Social Workers* 3: 3–14.

Mann, Philip. 1972. "Accessibility and Organizational Power in the Entry Phase of Mental Health Consultation." *Journal of Consulting Clinical Psychology* 38: 215–18.

—— 1973. "Student Consultants—Evaluation by Consultees." *American Journal of Community Psychology* 1: 182–93.

Mannino, Fortune V. 1964. "Developing Consultation Relationships with Community Agents." *Mental Hygiene* 48: 356–62.

—— 1970. *Perception of Consultation by Consultants and Consultees.* Adelphi, Md., Mental Health Study Center, National Institute of Mental Health; mimeo.

—— 1972. "Task Accomplishments and Consultation Outcome." *Community Mental Health Journal* 8: 102–8.

—— and Milton F. Shore. 1971. *Consultation Research in Mental Health and Related Fields—a Critical Review of the Literature,* Public Health General Publication 2122. Washington, D.C., United States Government Printing Office.

—— 1975. "Effecting Change through Consultation." In Fortune V. Mannino, Beryce W. MacLennan, and Milton F. Shore, eds., 25–48, *The Practice of Mental Health Consultation,* pp. 25–48. Adelphi, Md., National Institute of Mental Health.

—— 1975. "The Effects of Consultation—a Review of Empirical Studies." *American Journal of Community Psychology,* 3: 1–21.

May, C. R. 1970. "Community Mental Health Consultation in a Public Agency." *Public Welfare* 28: 150–57.

Mayer, Roy. 1972. "Relevance and Consulting—Using Behavior Modification Procedures in the Consulting Relationship." *Elementary School Guidance and Counseling* 7: 114–19.

Mazade, Noel A. 1972. "An Analysis of Community Mental Health Consultation—Education Programs Originating from Three Organization Structures," Unpublished Ph.D. dissertation, University of Pittsburgh School of Social Work.

—— 1974. "Consultation and Education Practice and Organization Structure in 10 Community Mental Health Centers." *Hospital and Community Psychiatry* 25: 673–75.

Meyers, Joel. 1975. "Consultee-centered Consultation with a Teacher as a Technique in Behavior Management." *American Journal of Community Psychology* 3: 111–21.

——, Michael P. Friedman, and Edward S. Gaughan. 1975. "The Effects of Consultee-centered Consultation on Teacher Behavior." *Psychology in the Schools* 12: 288–95.

Millar, T. P. 1966. "Psychiatric Consultation with Classroom Teachers." *Journal of the American Academy of Child Psychiatry* 5: 134–44.

Moed, George, and Donald Muhich. 1972. "Some Problems and Parameters of Mental Health Consultation." *Community Mental Health Journal* 8: 232–39.

Moore, Madeline U. 1938. "Psychiatric Services in Case Work Agencies." *The Family* 19: 216–23.

Morice, H. O. 1968. "The School Psychologist as a Behavioral Consultant: a Project in Behavior Modification—a Public School Setting." *Psychology in the Schools* 5: 253–61.

Morrison, A. P. 1970. "Consultation and Group Processes with Indigenous Neighborhood Workers." *Community Mental Health Journal* 6: 3–12.

Morrison, Thomas L., and Duane M. Thomas. 1975. "Educators and Child Case Workes' Perception about the Competencies of Mental Health Professionals." *Journal of Community Psychology* 3: 266–69.

Moss, Alice F. 1976. "Consultation in the Intercity Schools." *Social Work* (March) 142–46.

Musto, D. F. 1975. "Whatever Happened to Community Mental Health?" *The Public Interest* (Spring) 53–79.

Nagler, Sylvain, and Patrick Cook. 1973. "Some Ideological Considerations Underlying a Mental Consultation Program in Public Schools." *Community Mental Health Journal* 9: 244–52.

National Conference of Social Work. 1935. *Proceedings of the National Conference of Social Work* (formerly National Conference of Charities and Corrections) *Index 1874–1933*. Chicago, University of Chicago Press.

Neleigh, Janice R., et al. 1971. *Training Non-professional Community Porject Leaders,* Community Mental Health Monograph Series No. 6. New York, Behavioral Publications.

Newmann, Frederika. 1945. "The Use of Psychiatric Consultation by a Casework Agency." *The Family* 26: 137–42.

Nir, Y. 1973. "Consultation to Schools in Poverty Areas." *Child Welfare* 52: 425–30.

Nitzberg, Harold, and Marvin Kahn. 1962. "Consultation with Welfare Workers in a Mental Helath Clinic." *Social Work* 7: 84–93.

Norman, Edward C., and Theresa Forti. 1972. "A Study of the Process and Outcome of Mental Health Consultation." *Community Mental Health Journal* 8: 261–70.

Ormsby, Ralph. 1950. "Group Psychiatric Consultation in a Family Casework Agency." *Social Casework* 31: 361–65.

Pargament, Kenneth I. 1977. "A Police Department's Uninvited Guest: a Model for Initiating Consultative Entry into Human Service Organizations." *Journal of Community Psychology* 5: 75–85.

Parker, Beulah. 1962. "Some Observations on Psychiatric Consultation with Nursery School Teachers." *Mental Hygiene* 46: 559–66.

—— 1968. *Mental Health In-service Training.* New York, International Universities Press.

Pasnau, Robert, ed. 1975. *Consultation-Liaison Psychiatry.* New York, Grune and Stratton.

Perkins, George. 1958. "Psychiatric Consultation in Residential Treatments." *American Journal of Orthopsychiatry* 28: 266–75.

Perlmutter, Felice. 1974. "Prevention and Treatment: a Strategy for Survival." *Community Mental Health Journal* 10: 276–81.

—— and Herbert A. Silverman. 1973. "Conflict in Consultation-Education." *Community Mental Health Journal* 9: 116–22.

Plog, Stanley C. 1974. "Effectiveness, Leadership and Consultation."in *In The Workshop of Mental Health Consultation*, pp. 49–69. Washington, D.C., National Technical Information Service, U.S. Department of Commerce.

—— and Walter L. Ross. 1973. "The Status of Mental Health Consultation in the Schools." In *Mental Health Consultation to the Schools: Directions for the Future*, pp. 63–86. Washington, D.C., National Technical Information Service, U.S. Department of Commerce.

Polenz, Donald G. "Supervision and Consultation in Child Care Licensing: Special Reference to Children's Institutions." Unpublished Ph.D. dissertation, University of Southern California.

Rabiner, C. S., and S. Silberberg. 1970. "Consultation or Direct Service?" *American Journal of Psychiatry* 126: 1321–25.

Ramirez-Murgado, Jorge O. 1975. "Consultation and Education in a Chicano Community." *Social Casework* 56: 558–61.

Randolph, D. L. 1972. "Behavioral Consultation as a Means of Introducing the Quality of a Counseling Program." *School Counselor* 20: 30–35.

Rapoport, Lydia. 1963. "Consultation: an Overview." In Lydia Rapoport, ed., *Consultation in Social Work Practice*, New York: National Association of Social Workers.

—— 1965. "Consultation." In Harry L. Lurie, ed., *Encyclopedia of Social Work*, pp. 214–19. New York, National Association of Social Workers.

—— 1971*a*. "Book Review—the Theory and Practice of Mental Health Consultation, G. Caplan." *Social Service Review* 45: 223–24.

—— 1971*b*. "Consultation." In Robert Morris, ed., *Encyclopedia of Social Work*, pp. 156–61. New York, National Association of Social Workers.

——, ed. 1963. *Consultation in Social Work Practice*. New York, National Association of Social Workers.

Regensberg, Jeanette. 1951. "Utilizing the Contribution of Psychiatric Staff within an Agency." *Social Casework* 32: 231–36.

Reisinger, James John, John P. Ora, and George Frangia. 1976. "Parents as Change Agents for Their Children—a Review." *Journal of Community Psychology* 4: 103–23.

Reppucci, N. Dickon, *et al.* 1973. "We Bombed in Mountville: Lessons Learned in Consultation to a Correctional Facility for Adolescent Offenders." In Ira Goldenberg, ed., *The Helping Professions in the World of Action. I.* Lexington, Mass., Lexington Books.

Reschly, Daniel S. 1976. "School Psychology Consultation: 'Frenzied, Faddish or Fundamental.' " *Journal of School Psychology* 14: 105–13.

Rieman, Dwight W. 1963. "Group Mental Health Consultation with Public Nurses." In Lydia Rapoport, ed., *Consultation in Social Work Practice*, pp. 85–97. New York, National Association of Social Workers.

Riley, Mary Jean. 1958. "Psychiatric Consultation in Residential Treatment—the Child Care Worker's View." *American Journal of Orthopsychiatry* 28: 283–88.

Robbins, Paul R., and Esther C. Spencer. 1968. "A Study of the Consultation Process." *Psychiatry* 31: 362–68.

——, and Daniel A. Frank. 1970. "Some Factors Influencing the Outcome of Consultation." *American Journal of Public Health* 60: 524–34.

Roberts, Robert W. 1968. "Some Impressions of Mental Health Consultation in a Poverty Area." *Social Casework* 49: 339–45.

Robins, Arthur. 1964. "The Foreign Consultant's Role in Newly Developing Countries." In *Studies in Asia*, pp. 1–12. Lincoln, University of Nebraska Press.

Rogers, Ken Q. 1973. "Notes on Organization Consulting to Mental Hospitals." *Bulletin of the Menninger Clinic* 37: 211–31.

Rogawski, Alexander. 1974. "Mental Health Programs in Welfare Systems." In Arieti Silvano, ed., *American Handbook of Psychiatry*, Vol. II, pp. 750–72. New York, Basic Books.

Rosenthal, Maurice J., and Mary E. Sullivan. 1959. *Psychiatric Consultation in a Public Child Welfare Agency*, U.S. Children's Bureau Publication No. 372. Washington, D.C., Superintendent of Documents.

Rowitch, S. 1968. "Group Consultation with School Personnel." *Hospital and Community Psychiatry* 29: 261–66.

Ruckhaber, Charles. 1975. "Four Year Study of Psychological Consultation Process." *Psychology in the Schools* 12: 64–70.

Rumrill, M. S. 1957. "The Supervisor and the Consultant." *Nursing Outlook* 5: 164–65.

Savage, W. W. 1952. *Educational Consultants and Their Work in Midwestern State Departments of Education*. Chicago, University of Chicago.

Scheidlinger, Saul, Elmer L. Struening, and Judith G. Rabkin. 1970. "Evaluation of a Mental Health Consultation Service in a Ghetto Area." *American Journal of Psychotherapy* 24: 485–93.

Schein, Edgar H. 1969. *Process Consultation: Its Role in Organizational Development*. Reading, Mass., Addison-Wesley Publishing Co.

Schild, Judith S., Carla B. Scott, and D. Jane Zimmerman. 1976. "The Child Welfare Agency as School Consultant." *Child Welfare* 55: 491–500.

Schmuck, R. A. 1968. "Helping Teachers Improve Classroom Group Processes." *Journal of Applied Behavioral Science* 4: 401–35.

Seashore, Charles, and Elmer Van Egmond. 1961. "The Consultant-Trainer Role." In Warren G. Bennis, Kenneth D. Benne, and Robert Chin, eds., *The Planning of Change*, pp. 660–66. Holt, Rinehart and Winston.

Siegel, Doris. 1955. "Consultation: Some Guiding Principles." In *Administration, Supervision and Consultation*, pp. 98–114. New York, Family Service Association of America.

Signell, Karen and Patricia Scott. 1971. "Mental Health Consultation—

an Interaction Model." *Community Mental Health Journal* 7: 288–302.

—— 1972. "Training in Consultation: a Crisis-Role Transition." *Community Mental Health Journal* 8: 149–60.

Sikkema, Mildred. 1955. "The School Social Worker Serves as a Consultant." In *Casework Papers 1955,* pp. 75–82. New York, Family Service Association of America.

Silverman, Wade H. 1974. "Some Factors Related to Consultee Satisfaction with Consultation." *American Journal of Community Psychology* 2: 303–10.

Simon, E. L. 1966. "Medical Consultation in a County Welfare Department." *Public Welfare* 24: 274–77.

Simon, Herbert. 1965. *Administrative Behavior—a Study of Decision-making Processes in Administrative Organization.* 2d ed. New York, Free Press.

Smith, Joanne M. B. 1975. "Social Work Consultation—Implications for Social Work Education." Unpublished dissertation, University of Utah, Salt Lake City.

Smyth, Wilma. 1960. "Preventative Aspects of Medical Social Work Consultation in a Rural State." *Social Work* 5: 91–96.

Social Service Review. 1968. "Forty-Year Index." *Social Service Review* 42 (whole issue).

Spencer, Esther C. and H. T. Croley. 1963. "Administrative Consultation." In Lydia Rapoport, ed., *Consultation in Social Work Practice,* pp. 51–68. New York, National Association of Social Workers.

Splete, Howard H. 1968. "A Study of the Significant Elements of the Elementary School Counselor's Consultant Behavior as It Relates to Classroom Teachers. Unpublished Ph.D. dissertation, Michigan State University, East Lansing.

Stechler, Gerald. 1974. "Differential Approaches to Rural and Inner City Consultation." In *The Workshop on Mental Health,* pp. 81–92. Washington, D.C., National Technical Information Service, U.S. Department of Commerce.

Stein, Herman. 1956. "The Use of the Consultants." *American Journal of Orthopsychiatry* 26: 249–51.

Stelle, Fritz. 1973. *Consulting for Organizational Change.* Amherst, Mass., University of Massachusetts Press.

Stephenson, Susan D. 1973. "Judging the Effectiveness of a Consultation Program to a Community Agency." *Community Mental Health Journal* 9: 253–59.

Stevenson, George, and Geddes Smith. 1934. *Child Guidance Clinics—a Quarter of a Century of Development.* New York: Commonwealth Fund.

Stringer, Lorene A. 1961. "Consultation: Some Expectations, Principles and Skills." *Social Work¨* –90.

Tannenbaum, David E. 1951. "Establishing Psychiatric Consultation for Agency Program." *Social Casework* 32: 196.

Taylor, Joseph. 1956. "Psychiatric Consultation in Family Counseling." *Marriage and Family Living* 18: 259–62.

Tetreault, J. M. 1968. "Informal Consultation: Social Work Activity with the Elementary School Teacher." *Smith College Studies in Social Work* 39: 85–86.

Thomas, Addie. 1955. "New Approaches to Old Problems." *Medical Social Work* 4: 3–5.

Thompson, W. C. 1957. "Psychiatric Consultation in Social Agencies." *Child Welfare* 36: 1–3.

Thorne, Melvyn. 1975. "Foreword." *Special Issue Health Education Monographs* (Winter) 359–60.

Tilles, S. 1961. "Understanding the Consultant's Role." *Harvard Business Review* 39: 87–99.

Tobiessen, Jon, and Amnon Shai. 1971. "A Comparison of Individual and Group Mental Health Consultation with Teachers." *Community Mental Health Journal* 7: 218–26.

Towle, Charlotte. 1970. "The Consultation Process—Source Material." *Social Service Review* 44: 205–14.

Townsel, Lee E., John Irving, and Hans M. Stroo. 1975. "Mobile Consultation." *Social Work in Health Care* 1: 81–92.

Tyler, Marvin, and Milton Fine. 1974. "The Effects of United and Internal School Psychologist-Teacher Consultation." *Journal of School Psychology* 12: 8–16.

Ulmer, R. A., and S. C. Kupferman. 1970. "An Empirical Study of the Process and Outcome of Psychiatric Consultation." *Journal of Clinical Psychology* 26: 323–26.

United Nations. 1968. *Manual on the Use of Consultants in Developing Countries.* New York, United Nations.

United States Department of Health, Education and Welfare, National

Institute of Mental Health. 1975. *Provisional Data on Federally Funded Community Mental Health Centers.* Washington, D.C., Division of Biometry, Survey and Reports Branch.

Vacher, Carole D., and Nicholas E. Stratas. 1976. *Consultation-Education: Development and Evaluation.* New York, Human Sciences Press.

Van Driel, Agnes. 1942. "Consultation in Relation to the Administration of Social Service Programs." In *Consultation.* Menasha, Wis., George Banta Publishing Co.

Van Ophuijsen, J. H. W. 1940. "The Psychiatric Consultation." *American Journal of Orthopsychiatry* 19: 397–403.

Volenstein, A. F. 1955. "Some Principles of Psychiatric Consultation." *Social Casework* 36: 253–56.

Warren, Roland L. 1963. *Social Research Consultation—an Experiment in Health and Welfare Planning.* New York, Russell Sage Foundation.

Warringer, A. 1949. "The Psychiatric Social Worker as a Consultant." *Public Health Nursing* 41: 392–97.

White, Grace. 1947. "Medical Social Work." In *Social Work Yearbook, 1947.* New York, Russell Sage Foundation.

Williams, M. 1971. "The Problem Profile Technique in Consultation." *Social Work* 16: 52–59.

Wolfe, Harvey E. 1966. "Consultation Role, Function and Process." *Mental Hygiene* 50: 132–34.

Wood, Thomas L. 1973. "Social Work Consultation and Student Training in Day Care Centers." *Child Welfare* 52: 663–68.

Woodward, Luther E., ed. 1960. *Psychiatric Social Workers and Mental Health.* New York, National Association of Social Workers.

Woody, Robert H. 1974. "Forms of Mental Health Consultation." *Journal of Community Psychology* 2: 283–85.

—— 1975. "Process and Behavioral Consultation." *American Journal of Community Psychiatry* 3: 277–85.

—— and Jane D. Woody. 1971. "Behavioral Science Consultation." *Personnel Journal* 50: 382–91.

Wright, Benjamin. 1958. "Psychiatric Consultation in Residential Treatment: the Psychologist's View." *American Journal of Orthopsychiatry* 28: 276–82.

Zander, Alvin, Arthur Cohen, and Ezra Stotland. 1966. "Accommo-

dative Relationships—Psychiatry, Clinical Psychology, Social Work."
In Howard M. Vollmer and Donald L. Mills, eds., *Profes-
sionalization*, pp. 237–440. Englewood Cliffs, N.J., Prentice-Hall.
Zusman, Jack, and David Davidson. 1972. *Practical Aspects of Mental
Health Consultation*. Springfield, Ill., Charles Thomas.
Zwick, M. 1975. "Mental Health Consultation to Schools." *Social Work*
20: 145–47.

Index